Clicking
Through

Jonathan Ezor

Clicking Through

A SURVIVAL GUIDE FOR BRINGING YOUR COMPANY ONLINE

BLOOMBERG PRESS

PRINCETON

This publication contains the author's opinions and is designed to provide accurate and authoritative information. It is sold with the understanding that the author, publisher, and Bloomberg L.P. are not engaged in rendering legal, accounting, investment-planning, or other professional advice. The reader should seek the services of a qualified professional for such advice; the author, publisher, and Bloomberg L.P. cannot be held responsible for any loss incurred as a result of specific investments or planning decisions made by the reader.

First edition published 2000

3 5 7 9 10 8 6 4 2

Ezor, Jonathan.

Clicking through : a survival guide for bringing your company online / by Jonathan Ezor.

p.   cm.

"Webliography": P.   .

Includes index.

ISBN 1-57660-073-4

1. Industrial management -- Computer networks. 2. Electronic commerce. I. Title. II. Title: Survival guide for bringing your company online.

HD30.37.E97   2000

658'.05---dc21

99-41688

CIP

EDITED BY
Maris Williams

To my father, Edwin Lionel Ezor,

who taught me how to dream...

and how to write

—J.E.

ACKNOWLEDGMENTS

THIS BOOK IS LIKE THE INTERNET ITSELF: A COOPERATIVE effort of many individuals working behind the scenes. Most importantly, my wife, Stacy, and my sons Avi and Eitan have given me the time and encouragement to write and to do the work behind *Clicking Through*, and really made it possible. Next is my long-time colleague and friend Sheri F. London, Esq., who has been my counselor and "cheerleader" in this and many other projects.

I must also acknowledge Andrea Pedolsky and Nicholas Smith of Altair Literary Agency, who shared my vision for this book and found it a great "home" at Bloomberg. The thousands of real and virtual members of the World Wide Web Artists' Consortium and professionals such as John Moccia of The Rollins Agency and Elizabeth Lascoutx of CARU have been my invaluable teachers, to whom I owe a debt of thanks. Finally, to Michael Laudor, my best man and adviser in countless ways—be well, Michael.

Introduction

TECHNOLOGY HAS ALWAYS REPRESENTED THE DICH-
otomy of tremendous opportunity and significant
risk for businesses. From fire to the steam engine to
the fax machine, each new methodology or
invention has had its evangelists and its critics.
Technology itself is without moral values; it is an
extension and an enhancement of other activities. It
is a set of tools, not an ideology.

Historically, new technologies have done two
things. First, they have altered existing industries,
enhancing speed and efficiency, opening up new
markets, and increasing competitiveness. At the
same time, technological developments have also
created entirely *new* products and industries—
from genetically engineered pharmaceuticals to
900-number chat lines to overnight air delivery
services. Of course, technology has also served to
make some industries obsolete—the example of
the buggy whip at the dawn of the automotive age

is as clichéd as it is instructive.

The growth of the technology known as the Internet, however, is like nothing ever seen before. It isn't hyperbole to say that the speed and worldwide scope of the Internet and its relevance not only to businesses but also to the mass market is without precedent. The opportunities to businesses of every size and shape are unprecedented as well.

Most of the companies adopting the Internet as a business tool are entering into a whole new line of operation—whether or not they realize it. Bringing a business onto the Internet, perhaps by creating a Web site to advertise a product or to sell directly to consumers or other businesses, is an exercise in international digital publishing or broadcasting which instantly reaches millions of potential consumers. It's difficult to imagine that a bicycle parts manufacturer, for example, has completely thought out the ramifications of becoming a worldwide content publisher, or can even determine and take into account what the potential risks might be. It wants to use the Internet to sell brake cables to riders in the United States—but a Web site does much more than that.

Business managers, of course, are not strangers to risk assessment and management. A tremendous amount of time and money is spent every year to quantify and reduce (or insure against) risk of market turnaround, product failure, shifting trends, or unforeseen accidents. What happens, though, when a business owner doesn't even realize that a whole new category of risk has been added to the business? Without adequate preparation, the results can be disastrous.

This book is written primarily for managers and entrepreneurs who may not have experience in technology or international media. It will also be useful for anyone who is interested in how the Internet changes the legal and business environment for companies. Within these chapters you will find real strategies for evaluating, reducing, and ultimately effectively managing the business risks of creating a Web site, connecting employees to the Internet, and selling goods or services online.

To be in a position to leverage these opportunities, you need a basic understanding of what's really occurring when the button is pushed or the site is launched along with a reasonable amount of strategic planning. *Clicking Through* will serve as a practical reference for any company considering making the leap onto the Internet to start, grow, or leverage new or potential business. It will also present examples of companies in a variety of industries which have identified, managed, and successfully avoided the risks of being online, allowing them to reap the real rewards of the Internet as a business environment.

JONATHAN EZOR

CHAPTER 1

Preparing Your Company for E-Commerce

SPINNING THE WEB FOR BUSINESS

ERE'S A BIT OF COMFORT FOR the technophobes out there—this is not a book that requires an engineering or computer science degree. At the same time, though, it's important to have a basic idea of what the Internet is, and how it works.

The Internet was not designed as a commercial medium. In fact, until fairly recently (1991), the official policy of the U.S. government agencies responsible for originally creating and subsidizing the Internet was to prohibit commercial use except in very limited circumstances. As this policy changed and government subsidies diminished, industry stepped in to provide the traffic and revenue to keep the network operating for the consumer.

The Internet works very much like the international telephone "system," which connects companies and governments operating and maintaining telephone wires and switches all over the world. Customers pay service charges to the local companies that share those revenues in a fairly complicated series of usage fees with the other systems that carry calls beyond the local boundaries. And, of course, there are companies that own their internal wiring, and individuals who own telephones connected to the wiring. The same is true of the Internet, where many different entities own pieces of the network, and where revenues from usage fees on the local level are shared up the chain with larger network providers both in the United States and overseas.

The Internet significantly differs from the telephone networks in how it transmits information.

The Internet does not establish direct links between its users, or dedicate circuits to a particular message or Web page being sent across the network. When a message is sent across the Internet, it is broken up into pieces of a fixed size called "packets." Each of these packets contains a portion of the message, as well as information about the sender, the recipient, and the message. Each packet is sent separately, finding the route from origin to destination that has the least congestion.

Each message packet may take a different route. When the packets all get to where they're going, they meet, reassemble in the order indicated by their packet information, and become a single message again. The process was designed in part for situations such as nuclear war in which a direct connection for a message might be broken or unreliable—the network would detect the outage and redirect packets around the blackout area.

In theory, this distributed communications network is extremely reliable. In practice, though, much has changed since the protocols and routing processes were designed. Historically, the computers connected to the Internet were mainframes on academic campuses or in government facilities, capable of performing the routing as well as providing access to the Internet for their users. Most of the computers attached to the Internet today, though, are personal computers incapable of routing. The Internet service providers themselves do it, but they are servicing many customers, with much more traffic than ever before. Also, the protocols themselves were not designed for the tremendous amount of traffic carried by today's Internet, and much of the software is maintained and operated by quite fallible human beings. *risk* The result? Occasionally, the network can experience significant outages, or at least delays, particularly when a number of problems occur at once. Still, the Internet's infrastructure means that the network never actually crashes entirely, just slows—and that as soon as problems are resolved, the back traffic continues on its way. Overloaded as it may be, the system still works.

The international scope of the Internet is another vital fact to keep in mind. Unlike a telephone call, in which the sender knows exactly to whom the call is being placed, putting publicly available material on the Internet makes it immediately available to users literally everywhere in the world simultaneously. The Internet has no boundaries, and for now there are only limited and unreliable means of detecting from which country a particular user hails.

Knowing the nature of the Internet gives us a framework for evaluating rewards and for addressing, reducing, and ultimately surmounting the risks involved in Internet-based business. As subsequent chapters will show, this process will involve technical expertise, solid contracts, appropriate structuring of the business, and more traditional risk management methods such as liability insurance.

Now let's take an initial look at some of the Internet's commercial uses.

Advertising

BUSINESSES USE WEB SITES FOR MANY DIFFERENT PURPOSES. The earliest commercial function of Web sites was to advertise companies and products. When there were relatively few sites on the Internet, just launching one was enough to get publicity and an audience, especially if the site was the first for a particular industry. Over time the promotional aspect of Web sites has not diminished, but rather, has broadened, with hundreds of thousands of sites serving many advertising purposes, such as:

◆ carrying a branding message
◆ running an online contest or sweepstakes
◆ showing print or broadcast advertisements as part of the site's content
◆ providing more detailed information on the business and its products than is commonly available in traditional advertisements (where space and/or time is at a premium).

It's still possible to garner press coverage for a novel advertisement element, particularly one that has particular entertainment or utility value.

Interaction and Information

VERY EARLY ON, BUSINESSES UNDERSTOOD THAT THE MAJOR difference between the Internet and traditional media was the Net's interactivity—customers could not only be reached, but they could also reach back, whether through e-mail, a Web site's chat area, or even live voice and video-conferencing over a computer connection. Customers soon realized that it was faster to type a request into a computer system via a Web site than to locate a customer service representative on the telephone and wait while the representative typed (or often mistyped) information, then reported the answer. It took a few years following this realization, though, before the technology and average bandwidth available to users could properly integrate the interactive elements in most commercial Web sites.

Online retailers have added interactive databases to their Web sites to increase convenience and (more importantly) to save money in telemarketing and customer support services. Users are now able to find the nearest store by typing in an area code or zip code, get up-to-the-minute prices on goods, and check whether a desired item is in stock anywhere with-

At Your (Automated) Service, Sir

AMONG THE EARLIEST and still most popular interactive features is the ability for a consumer to directly access the company's databases for specific information, without having to speak with a customer service representative. Federal Express was a pioneer in this area, allowing its customers to track packages in real time simply by typing an air bill number into an online form (or sending the number via e-mail), and United Parcel Service and the U.S. Postal Service soon followed suit. Many Web sites also make "Frequently Asked Questions" (or FAQ) documents available, to answer most customers' troubleshooting or simple usage questions without requiring the aid of a live operator.

in the store's network of locations. The novelty is not the information itself, but the fact that consumers can get to it at home or in the office at any hour, without having to wait on hold for a customer service representative.

The database services that benefit consumers have an even greater impact in the business-to-business arena. With the complicated nature of today's global economy, it is critical for everyone from parts suppliers to manufacturers to retailers to know where specific goods are in the "channel." Previously these requests were handled by fax, telephone, and telex requests that required human response and forced everyone to cooperate on a proprietary, often expensive, common network of hardware and software. The Internet allows this process to operate independently and automatically. Not only can individual users type in requests for information, but it's fairly simple to build computerized trackers operating over the Internet using commonly available software tools. No business needs to change its inventory control system to suit its channel partners; all it takes is integrating the existing system into a Web server.

Online Commerce

INFORMATION IS ONE THING—WHAT ABOUT PHYSICAL goods? Being able to deliver actual goods based on a Web site order form is a wonderful thing, since it can empower customers to examine catalog information, check whether the desired item is in stock, fill out an address form, and pay for the order, all without the need for human assistance. Additionally, a customer shopping online can quickly get more product information than a retailer's site may provide, perhaps through a link to the manufacturer's own site, then come back with a mouse click to complete the purchase. With the right software, the customer can select items for a "shopping cart," making a single joint purchase at a later hour or day, and may be able to store a delivery address and credit card number once and reuse it securely.

Online retailing does have a few limitations. First, there are real issues of security involved, since the Internet is a public network. Selling may require you to collect not only name and address information, which itself is sensitive, but credit card or other financial data as well. In order for this collection to be both safe and convenient, software for scrambling the transmission of information between customer and company had to be developed and made widely available. Today, encryption technology is contained within the vast majority of Web browser and server software. (Encryption is discussed in more detail later in this chapter.)

Another element required for successful online commerce is actually making the goods viewable and available via the Web site, in at least as convenient and complete a form as the paper catalogs with which Web sites compete. (In some cases, from music to software to books, the goods may even be directly deliverable via the Web, a faster and often cheaper method than a regular shipment.) The earliest Web site catalogs were subsets of the total product list available from vendors such as Lands' End <http://www.lands end.com> or The Sharper Image <http://www.sharper image.com>. By integrating databases into online catalogs, and by entering the names and images of all or at least the most popular products, online vendors have vastly improved the quality and usability of their sites. Many of the same issues involving security, completeness, and responsiveness are being faced and addressed by nonretail businesses. The Web is an incredibly flexible medium for commercial use. With its combination of novel technologies and widely adopted standard protocols and software, the Web offers businesses many different ways to make or save money, or do both at the same time. These opportunities exist not just for technology companies, but also for small businesses in all industries, because the audience of the Web is a broadening demographic of local and international users.

When it comes to risk management on a Web site, though, the numerous options for format and function mean that many possible risk situations must be considered. There are several major categories of potential problems, which we will discuss in subsequent chapters. Among these are content liability, privacy and confidentiality, and

consumer protection. The risks arising out of these areas—
from laws and regulations, court decisions, treaties and contracts, and public perception—must be considered when
you decide whether and how your particular business will
use the World Wide Web as a tool to reach customers and
suppliers.

BUILDING YOUR WEB SITE

WHILE THE INTERNET MAY HAVE MANY BUSINESS APPLICA-
tions, most business owners will limit their use of the Internet to their company Web site.

Here are some recognizable companies whose online ventures have paid off:

Large retailers from Macy's to Service Merchandise to
Lands' End, right down to the smallest Web-only specialty
store, are publishing catalogues and making sales online.

Delivery companies such as UPS, Federal Express, and the
U.S. Postal Service are saving on toll-free customer service
costs by allowing users to directly check the status of packages via a Web site.

Stockbrokers are finding the same savings and increasing
their business dramatically through online trading and
research features.

Information vendors and analysts such as Forrester
Research and the Gartner Group are publishing their reports
online, with executive summaries available to the public and
full data on a subscription-only basis.

Traditional publishers such as the *New York Times* and *The
Wall Street Journal* are reprinting their content online, finding new subscribers and advertising revenue and (in the case
of the *Journal* and *Consumer Reports* magazine) subscription
fees as well.

Search engines and Web indexes (like Hotbot or Yahoo!)
and online communities (<http://ParentsPlace.com> and
thousands of others) are springing up as fast as someone can
put an idea together with a developer.

No matter what a site is designed to do, businesses face a

number of risks when building Web sites. Creating and hosting the site poses potential problems, so we will turn our attention there next.

Hiring a Web Developer

BASIC WEB SITE DESIGN IS NOT DIFFICULT. THERE ARE COUNTLESS software packages, many available for free or low cost, that will shield a businessperson from the complexities of the Hypertext Markup Language (HTML) which establishes the display and formatting of a simple Web site. As online commerce has grown, Web site designers have had to create more accessible and exciting sites to attract consumers. It is because of this increased competition that fewer business owners are do-it-yourself Web site designers. Most companies turn to contractors, such as advertising agencies or dedicated Web shops, to design and build their Internet presences.

Hiring an outside contractor to design your Web site can be done in two ways: The first way is to hire an agency, just as you would for a print ad, to design and implement creative promotional materials as a "work made for hire." Most advertising is therefore owned free and clear by the client, and the agency keeps no rights to reuse or resell its own creative work. The second model comes from the software industry, which has grown up around the principle of "licensing." In most software development, the developer will retain copyright (ownership) to the code, and the client will receive only a limited license to use the program. Often, even if the client wants to make changes or otherwise customize the software for its specific needs, it doesn't have the readable version of the program (called "source code") which would make that possible.

THE QUESTION OF OWNERSHIP

WEB SITES USUALLY CONSIST OF BOTH CREATIVE MATERIAL and software, so who owns the material that makes up a Web site? That depends on the type of contract you negotiate. U.S. copyright law provides that the creator of a work automatically holds the exclusive copyright to it. Therefore, the only way

Harvesting

WHAT CAN HAPPEN if ownership of a Web site or its content is not clearly established? One serious risk is the possibility of Web site "harvesting": one party, either the developer or the client, copies the live site down from the Internet to a local hard drive before the transaction is completed. When a customer does it, the developer may not get paid if the customer goes somewhere else to complete the work. When a developer does it, the developer may have enough technical knowledge to remove the site from the Internet after it is harvested, and the customer may be forced to pay the developer extra (or give in on a fee dispute) in order to retrieve the site and utilize it. "Harvesting" also refers to infringers who copy a site's elements to reuse them in another country or another language without permission.

that copyright may be transferred to a customer is in *writing* as part of a signed contract.

What happens if a business does not own the rights to its Web site? If the developer goes out of business, resigns the account, or is otherwise unsatisfactory, your company may not have the legal right to make further modifications to the site without the developer's permission. Even if you and your company have worked hand-in-hand with the developer in creating novel site ideas and implementation, the developer may be able to take those ideas and resell them, perhaps even to your chief competitor. Because the company's good will is at stake through the quality and timeliness of the Web site, it's important to maintain practical and legal control over the content of the site.

Putting It in Writing

THERE ARE MANY SITUATIONS IN WHICH ABSOLUTE OWNERship of a Web site is not necessary or even desirable. For instance, some highly sought-after developers are known for a particular skill or set of functions they provide to their clients, such as novel software or electronic commerce solutions. Those developers will probably not grant copyright to their unique elements. Insisting that they do so will prevent that developer from accepting your project. Other times, a developer may charge five or even ten times more if rights are transferred rather than a license being granted. Your company may not want to spend the extra money on the site, and it probably doesn't have to.

Before entering into a contract with a developer, you must first decide what kind of rights you and your company need to retain. It's crucial to read the language carefully to determine the proposed ownership division. The best approach is to analyze exactly what elements are going into the Web site, perhaps using a checklist, and to determine what your company will (or might) need to do with those elements both during and after your work with the developer. Then, negotiate ownership when you need it and license when you don't, and each party goes away from the deal satisfied that it retains what it needs to continue its business.

Most contracts will use the words "work for hire" or "work made for hire" to describe how the developer's work is to be owned by the customer. The U.S. copyright law's specific categories of what constitutes a "work made for hire," however, may not cover most third-party developer Web site projects. Even if the contract uses the words "work made for hire," the developer's product may not be legally owned by the customer. As a result, the ownership provision of the contract should state that if any materials to be treated as a "work made for hire" do not automatically belong to the company under the law, the developer will take the necessary legal steps to actually transfer ownership of the copyright.

Ownership of Third-Party Materials

ANOTHER WRINKLE TO COPYRIGHT OWNERSHIP OF TEXT AND graphics is the use of stock photos and other pre-existing works acquired from third parties. You may not receive ownership of such materials from the site developer, because the developer does not own the images, but may only license them on your behalf for limited purposes. Here, it is essential that the developer makes sure to acquire all rights necessary for your present and future use, especially the right to digitally transmit the images over the Internet. The developer must also take the necessary action to transfer these rights to you on or prior to delivery and launch of the final site.

Integrating Proprietary Software into a Web Site

SPECIAL SOFTWARE CAN MAKE YOUR WEB SITE MORE INTER-esting and may help introduce your product to customers. This software may perform animation, play video or music, connect the site with a database (for customer or purchase information, for example), or add security to the online communication. The software that a developer includes within a Web site will usually come from one of three sources: a third-party software vendor (such as Microsoft or Netscape), the preexisting library of the developer itself, or through custom development specifically for your company.

In the case of third-party software, the developer generally won't receive ownership, and therefore can only pass along the license it obtains from the vendor. That license must cover your proposed use, including the possibility that you might want to switch developers or operating systems or use the product across different business units or affiliates, and pricing will vary accordingly.

If the software comes from the developer's proprietary library, it is unlikely that your company will receive ownership of that code. After all, it is a part of the value of the developer's business, and may even be a reason why your company chose this developer over others. Again, a license is the most practical solution.

When software is custom developed, or existing software is heavily customized for your Web site, you may feel that because your project was the impetus for the product, your company should own it free and clear. On the other hand, it is likely that your company is not in the business of reselling Web site software or services, so you may not need the rights that come from ownership. The developer, though, may gain significant business value by the re-use of the software, and will be hesitant to give up ownership under any circumstances.

The key question in customized software for a Web site is the price of the developer's services. Many developers acknowledge the value they receive from re-use of newly written code, and will give the customer the option to pay either 100 percent of the development costs and own the copyright, or pay a discounted fee and settle for a license. For many companies, the latter option makes the most sense. If you choose this route, though, make sure not only that the license is of the appropriate scope, but that the developer agrees not to resell or license the software to your competitors. After all, why should your vision be allowed to work against you? Most developers will agree to reasonable restrictions on sales to competitors.

Another approach to negotiating the customized software is to create a joint venture. If the product created for the site has significant market value, your company may wish to join forces with the developer to commercialize and license the product to outside parties. Sometimes these deals can take the form of granting ownership to the developer but providing for a royalty to be paid to your company for each future sale (in order to allow you to receive a return on your financial and intellectual investment). These deals can be lucrative, but they add significant complication to the business relationship, since they force you and the developer to remain affiliated long after the site is finished, or even after the development itself has been terminated because of a dispute. You are also forced to rely on the sales and management skills of the developer, including the ability to actually get additional revenue from other customers. Further, royalty deals always require a fair amount of both trust and access to business records to ensure accurate and timely payment. If your company does not get its royalties, you may have to choose between litigation and taking the loss.

Ultimately, what makes sense for most nontechnology

businesses whose sites require customized software is to forego the royalty situation altogether and negotiate a broad license on fair economic terms. It is important to clarify whether the software is easily maintained and corrected by someone other than the developer, or whether you would need access to the underlying source code of the program if a problem arose and the developer were unavailable to fix it. In the event source code is needed, most developers will agree to a third-party escrow arrangement, which will protect their intellectual property from disclosure, but which will enable you (or another consultant you hire) to keep the system going if the developer goes out of business or can no longer support the product itself. The key to these arrangements is to look carefully at what each party actually needs to continue its business after the relationship between them ends, and come up with an appropriate cost for providing (or receiving) those rights. A reasonable developer will work with you to accomplish that goal.

The Remaining Pieces of the Ownership Puzzle

THERE ARE OTHER WEB SITE ELEMENTS WHOSE OWNERSHIP needs to be determined either in advance or as soon as their introduction is contemplated. Between software and creative work lies a broad midground of material which has qualities of both, including:

◆ HTML, CGI (common gateway interface) scripts, and Javascript for controlling the server computer
◆ Animation and games using tools such as Macromedia's Shockwave
◆ Java applets and Active X controls (small programs that run within Web browser software)

These are just some of the formatting and interactivity components which may be part of your Web site. How the developer treats them and whether you need to obtain ownership of them will depend on a few factors, including:

◆ The complexity and features of the element: the greater the

The Final Word on Ownership

YOU REALLY NEED to understand each of the pieces of your Web site in as much detail as possible. Specify in the agreement who will own and control each element. Remember, these pieces may include:

◆ text, graphics, audio, and video files provided by you

◆ third-party photos and other creative material (which may have talent rights involved)

◆ software created by the developer

◆ software created by third parties

◆ HTML, CGI, and other coding

The better you are at this process, the fewer conflicts you will have with your developer, particularly if the development process itself is interrupted or terminated for some reason.

complexity, and the more features it provides, the more likely the developer will wish to license rather than sell it

◆ Whether the developer used either a third-party product or something from its own library as part of the creation of the element: preexisting materials are usually licensed, not sold.

Once you determine whether or not you need ownership, be sure the contract states in depth how much detail you will require about how the element was created in order to keep the site going and add features and content to it.

Understanding the Risks of Misunderstanding

OWNERSHIP IS NOT THE ONLY RISK TO CONSIDER WHEN arranging for a site to be developed. The contract with the developer must also cover whether in fact you are getting what you are paying for. Often business owners are not technically savvy, and may not even know what questions to ask the developer, let alone how to understand the answers. For example, a company may have a fixed budget for the design of a Web site. Sites, though, are often more complicated than first thought, and it's not unusual for a company to discover late in the process that it isn't getting the features it absolutely needs.

Let's use fictional barbecue sauce vendor, BarBYou, which wants to expand onto the Internet as an example. Imagine that it is critical for BarBYou to track how many bottles are sold in each area code, because its distribution agreements require it. If that is not communicated clearly by BarBYou up front, the developer may price the site design without taking into account the ten hours of extra programming and the license fee for third-party software that this feature will require. By the time BarBYou finally becomes aware of the missing feature, the only choices may be to launch the site without the crucial function, or find money elsewhere to build it at the last minute, neither of which is particularly appealing. Suppose that BarBYou demands a high-tech graphic-rich site, with animation and movies showing care-free chefs at the grill, in the thought that it will be a better marketing move. Unless the company listens to the developer, though, it may not find out that such sites take so long to download into the average user's computer that no one will bother using the site in the first place.

It's not necessary or even recommended to leave the contracting process to the technical people within the company. They often do not understand the marketing or corporate motivations for the site. Rather, it's critical to get the input of everyone within the company who can contribute to a better understanding of both the needs being addressed by the Web site and what the developer is saying during the discussions. Then, after the site is properly fleshed out and the parties have a true understanding, the contract should go into sufficient detail to describe and formalize that understanding.

Agreeing on Specifications

IT IS CRITICAL THAT DETAILED WRITTEN SPECIFICATIONS be included within the contract in order to verify that both parties are aware of their obligations. If it is not possible to prepare specifications up front, because the project is evolving over time, provide the capability to add those specifications as they are finalized—then make sure that you add them to the contract.

Here are some of the elements you want to include in the specifications:

- Deliverables
- Deadlines
- Acceptance criteria
- Payment amounts and milestones
- Proprietary or third-party software being added to the project
- Any additional services which are desired or available from the developer, such as hosting (which will be addressed in the next section), ongoing maintenance of the site and its software, and advertising/PR services for the site or your company as a whole.

Maintaining Content and Software

MAINTENANCE CAN CREATE BUSINESS RISK THROUGH DIS-putes over areas of responsibility and quality of service. The term "maintenance" encompasses a whole litany of possible services, including minor or major updates to the content of the site, troubleshooting and solving technical problems, hardware service and support, and installation of updated software components. Many companies are quoted a price for maintenance without ever receiving clarification about which of these services are meant, and how much time the contractor is allocating for the quoted price. Often the arrangement will be for a fixed fee covering minor mainte-nance, such as small content updates (e.g., a press release), link-checking, and general troubleshooting. Significant redesigns or additions, installation, and consulting services may be charged by the hour or the day beyond the basic rate.

For the Web site designer, it is not easy to differentiate between minor and major updates, or come up with descrip-tions of services that everyone understands. This is why it's essential that the agreement give detailed information about the limitations on maintenance and the pricing for services beyond those limits.

Another common pitfall in the maintenance area is timing. Many developers carry a number of clients whose projects may have to be given priority over your company's needs. If the agreement does not delineate when a particular task needs to be given highest priority, a company may find itself unable to change its site even when facing regulatory sanctions or a costly error, simply because the developer has no one available to do it. Make sure that the agreement states which requests will be given high priority and that the developer tell you what response time the company can reasonably expect. For a critical update, you should be able to notify the developer and have the change done within one or two business days (assuming the change can be made in that time frame). What kinds of problems could arise? The following example may help:

Imagine that one of the pages of the BarBYou Web site lists the ingredients of the number-one selling condiment, BarB-YOW! Hot Sauce, but accidentally leaves out a spice to which a few people are sometimes fatally allergic. You can see how problematic it would be if the developer could not change the text for three weeks due to a backlog of client work. Since this sort of request needs much more immediate attention than a switch in background color of a page to match the bottle label, the contract should be drafted so that urgent requests such as this take precedence over design problems. The developer should use reasonable efforts to notify you when a requested critical path change will require longer repair time. The contract can also spell out how long noncritical changes will generally take. Finally, the contract should provide for a notification process, which keeps the relevant people at both the developer and your company aware of the critical change requests and the status of the efforts to make the changes.

CLOSING THE CONTRACT GAPS

AT LEAST THREE OTHER SECTIONS SHOULD BE A PART OF ANY site development negotiation and contract, or any services contract for that matter, in order to minimize business risk: term and termination, confidentiality of shared information, and warranties of performance.

TERM AND TERMINATION: HOW LONG BEFORE SAYING "SO LONG"

HOW LONG IS THIS PROJECT OR RELATIONSHIP EXPECTED TO continue, and under what circumstances will it end earlier than planned? In one common approach, each party has the right to terminate the relationship and the agreement if the other party breaches the contract in a material way and doesn't repair the breach after some amount of time stipulated in the provision itself. Many contracts provide for termination "for convenience," in order to allow a client (or even the developer) to simply end the relationship without cause on a certain amount of written notice. Most contracts also permit termination if one party or the other goes out of business, is bankrupt, or becomes insolvent. In addition to the conditions under which the agreement can be terminated, make sure you agree upon what happens after termination. For instance, who owns the material already created for the Web site? What has to be paid? The answers may differ depending on who terminates the deal, and whether it's for convenience or cause, but it will be easier to decide if you lay it out in a contract.

KEEPING QUIET: CONFIDENTIALITY OF BUSINESS INFORMATION

IN ORDER TO DO THE BEST JOB OF EMBODYING YOUR BUSI-ness in the site, the developer needs to understand your business. That will almost certainly require visits to your offices or factories, review of both marketing and corporate materials, and discussions of future products and service offerings, since there will be some lead time required to incorporate them into the site. For the developer, too, a good relationship may require disclosure of its proprietary technology, including some that may not be available or announced to the public. It's essential that each party be obligated to keep the other's information confidential, and only use it for the furthering of the business relationship. At the same time, there need to be limitations on those restrictions. Let the developer know how long your information must be kept confidential (most confidentiality obligations do not exceed five years from disclosure), and include a provision that states that material in the public domain or that has been independently developed or legitimately received from outside your company will not be considered confidential. These provisions are not unique to Web development agreements; any contract between two collaborating companies will usually have similar language.

PROMISES, PROMISES—WARRANTIES AND INDEMNIFICATION

WARRANTIES AND INDEMNIFICATION, A VERY IMPORTANT pair of contract sections, are entirely devoted to risk management. The infringement of intellectual property rights (copyright, trademark, or patent) is one such risk. It would be unfair for your company to ask the developer to accept responsibility if the annual report photos provided by you for the site could not be legally transmitted over the Internet. Similarly, the developer should not require your company to investigate every line of programming code to make sure it was not copied from another software company. Therefore, each party will probably warrant (a word for a promise with certain legal implications) that the materials it provides do not infringe any third party's rights.

As a matter of course, each party generally warrants that its agreement does not breach any other contract or arrangement to which it might be subject. Depending on contract responsibilities of each party, additional specific warranties might also be included. To confirm the understanding of the parties, and to make sure that no "implied" warranties are placed on a party by law or business practice without its knowledge, it is important to state that only the express written warranties in the contract itself will govern the relationship.

Indemnification is the flip side of warranties. If problems do arise because one party failed to prevent risks, and the other party is sued or suffers some other kind of financial or business harm, the party that failed to prevent the problem should take responsibility for the case and pay any judgment or damages to which the other company may be subject. This indemnification serves as an incentive for each party to actively manage and reduce any risks it can.

We have discussed the basic principles of the risk-management process for negotiating and drafting a contract. Of course, you aren't precluded from seeking legal redress if the Web developer injures your business, even if the contract does not specifically give you a remedy (although you should not agree to exclude any remedies you might later need if things go wrong). If your contract provides for a remedial process, however, you have a much better sense going into the deal of what might happen, and you reduce the need for costly litigation to settle a question that could easily have been resolved up front. Above all, consider what could possibly go wrong with the development process or the business relationship, and how likely the problems are to occur. After you have done this risk calculation, the contract should be written to place the risks on the party best able to avoid or minimize them, and the pricing of the deal can reflect not only the out-of-pocket costs in designing the Web site, but the business risk faced by each party as it enters into the business relationship. The better the calculation, the less likely you are to waste time in argument or litigation if disputes arise.

SAMPLE CONTRACT PROVISIONS— WEB DEVELOPMENT

Ownership by Customer

◆ **Ownership.** All content and other works relating exclusively to the Site developed by Developer in connection with this Agreement shall be deemed to be "works made for hire" under the Copyright Act of 1976 and the sole and exclusive property of BarBYou. BarBYou, at its sole expense, shall have the sole right to register such works for copyright protection. To the extent that these works shall for any reason be considered not to be a "work made for hire" for U.S. copyright law purposes, then Developer hereby conveys, transfers, and assigns all right, title, and interest it may have now or in the future acquire therein pertaining to the works to BarBYou, including but not limited to all copyrights and other intellectual property rights pertaining to the works, and agrees to execute all instruments necessary to accomplish such transfer and assignment at the sole expense of BarBYou and as requested by BarBYou.

Licensing Developer's Software

◆ **Software included in the site.** The computer programs known as SauceMerchant developed or provided by Developer hereunder ("Developer Programming") are not included in the works. As between BarBYou and Developer, the Developer Programming shall remain the sole and exclusive property of Developer. Developer hereby grants a worldwide, fully paid-up, perpetual, nonexclusive, transferable license to BarBYou to use, copy, perform, or display the object code for such Developer Programming, whether on hardware owned or controlled by Developer or otherwise, for the purpose of operating, maintaining, updating, supporting, and otherwise exploiting the Site.

Warranties and Indemnification

◆ **Developer warranties.** Developer warrants that it has all necessary rights and authority to execute and deliver this Agreement and perform its obligations hereunder and to grant the rights granted under this Agreement to BarBYou; that nothing contained in this Agreement or in the performance of this Agreement will place Developer in breach of any other contract or obligation; and that the provision of the works created by Developer to BarBYou for integration into the Site will not in any way constitute an infringement or other violation of any copyright, patent, trademark, trade secret, or other proprietary or personal rights of any third party. Developer makes no other warranty, express or implied, regarding the products or services to be provided by developer hereunder, including but not limited to any warranties of merchantability or fitness for a particular purpose.

◆ **BarBYou warranties.** BarBYou warrants that it has all necessary rights and authority to execute and deliver this Agreement and perform its obligations hereunder, and nothing contained in this Agreement or in the performance of this Agreement will place BarBYou in breach of any other contract or obligation; and that the provision of any materials by BarBYou to Developer for integration into the Site will not in any way constitute an infringement or other violation of any copyright, patent, trademark, trade secret, or other proprietary or personal rights of any third party.

◆ **Mutual indemnification.** Each party hereby indemnifies and shall defend and hold harmless the other party and its officers, directors, employees, and agents from and against all liability, damages, loss, cost, or expense (including but not limited to reasonable attorneys' fees and expenses) arising out of or in connection with any breach by the indemnifying party of its warranties hereunder. Upon the assertion of any claim or the commencement of any suit or proceeding against an indemnitee by any third party that may give rise to liability of an indemnitor hereunder, the indemnitee shall promptly notify the indemnitor of the existence of such claim (unless failure to give such prompt notice shall not materially prejudice the indemnitor's rights) and shall give the indemnitor reasonable opportunity to defend and/or settle the claim at its own expense and with counsel of its own selection. The indemnitee shall cooperate with the indemnitor, shall at all times have the right to fully participate in such defense at its own expense and shall not be obligated, against its consent, to participate in any settlement that it reasonably believes would have an adverse effect on its business. An indemnitee shall not make any settlement of any claims that might give rise to liability of an indemnitor hereunder without the prior written consent of the indemnitor.

Sample Specifications

Developer shall develop the site from comps and content provided by BarBYou, including graphics, text, and any audio or video clips, and write any custom scripts required to enable the interactive functions and database development. Developer will supply simple navigational elements (buttons) and hyperlinks. Developer will create all of the Hypertext Markup Language ("HTML") coding to enable the functionality of hyperlinks and file transfers (downloadable images, audio, and text). Developer will also write the necessary scripts to enable forms submissions, secure transactions, database links, searches, and e-mail submissions. Developer will develop the design and interactive logic for the Site.

Delivery of the initial components of the Site for BarB-You's acceptance shall occur no later than _____ with availability of the Site to the public to occur no later than _____ ("Publication"). It is agreed that BarB-You may, at its election, cancel this Agreement or any part hereof if such delivery and/or Publication does not occur within the time so specified. In the event of such cancellation, BarBYou shall pay only the verified direct costs incurred by Developer in the performance of Developer's obligations prior to such cancellation, provided, however, that the total amount of such costs shall not exceed the Development Fee.

Developer will network the Site throughout the Internet and help develop a strategy to integrate the site with BarB-You's overall marketing plan.

In the initial implementation Developer will develop the design direction and establish the architecture to support subsequent phases. Features may include animation, bulletin boards, e-mail and chat areas, downloadable audio and video clips.

Development Fee: Developer's fee for the Development Services shall be $_____.

A GRACIOUS HOST FOR YOUR SITE

WE HAVE LOOKED AT HOW A BUSINESS AND A DESIGNER collaborate to build a Web site. But what happens to the site after it's built? Simply put, it's placed on a computer connected to the Internet and published to the rest of the world in an ongoing process called *hosting*.

Just as Web site design runs the gamut from self-built pages to multimillion-dollar Web communities, hosting options also cover a broad spectrum. Some companies host their sites themselves on server computers that may also support the company's internal network. Beyond the security risks this may pose (beginning in Chapter 3), it forces a nontechnology business to manage an unfamiliar area of operations, without the economies of scale available to a hosting firm.

For most businesses with Web sites, the logical decision is to outsource to a hosting company. This allows the company to concentrate on its core business and to choose a hosting firm with the specific features it needs. Whether the host is the same company that developed the site or another firm concentrating its business exclusively on that end of the industry, there are risks and contract terms to manage.

Bandwidth

THERE ARE A FEW TERMS WITH WHICH YOU NEED TO BE familiar when shaping hosting arrangements. The first is *bandwidth*, the size of the electronic pipeline through which information flows in and out of your Web site. The higher the bandwidth, the faster your site will operate and the more likely you will be to sustain viewer interest.

Most hosting companies will charge you more for a higher level of bandwidth usage, perhaps on a sliding scale, reflecting their own increased costs to their service providers up the line.

An agreement from a hosting company often mentions maximum usage to which your site will be entitled, but not necessarily the minimum guaranteed bandwidth which will always be available for your use. This is critical, since most hosting companies make their money by contracting for a fixed amount of bandwidth which they then resell—the more companies they can contract with to share that bandwidth, the greater their profits. Think of it like a toll road— the local turnpike or freeway authority charges a toll to get on a superhighway, and says that drivers may go a maximum of 55 or 65 miles per hour. Usually, the greater the capacity of the highway and the more convenient its route, the higher the toll. However, no toll collector will ever guarantee that traffic, construction, or bad weather won't slow your car to 15 miles per hour, although the price of the toll doesn't change.

In a car, slow traffic can be an annoyance; with a business-critical Web site, not being given full use of the bandwidth

A Guide to Bandwidth
by Connection Options

OFTEN A HOSTING COMPANY or telecommunications provider will not directly state what kind of bandwidth it offers, but will describe options available through various types of lines. By means of comparison, the fastest generally accepted standard for data communications over a regular modem, V.90, offers 56Kbps (kilobits per second) receiving, and 33Kbps sending. Some of the higher bandwidth offerings include:

◆ **ISDN: Integrated Services Digital Network.** This type of connectivity uses existing copper phone lines of the POTS (Plain Old Telephone System) with special digital adapters to provide for up to 128Kbps of data transfer.

◆ **ADSL: Asymmetric Digital Subscriber Line.** This is a newly developed technology that (like ISDN) uses existing copper wires. When fully implemented, it may offer up to 8Mbps receiving and 1Mbps sending. Other DSL technologies are in implementation and more are under development.

◆ **T1 or DS1.** A special digital-only line that offers 1.544 Mbps (Megabits per second), which is equal to 1,544Kbps.

◆ **T3 or DS3.** A higher end (and more expensive) digital-only connection offering up to 45Mbps (45,000Kbps) connections.

You may also see references to "Fractional T1" or "Fractional T3"—this means that a number of computers (or companies) may be sharing a single line, dividing the available bandwidth in various ways. As we will see, just naming the type of connection doesn't guarantee or even establish the available bandwidth, but it at least gives the general parameters.

you think you have purchased can be devastating. Imagine if you're the second customer the hosting company has assigned to a given T1, and the first is Yahoo! or Microsoft (or any other highly accessed site). It's not at all assured that your site will get reasonable response times, because of the significant demands on available bandwidth by the other site using the line. In order to ensure you get what you need, make sure to include appropriate language in the hosting agreement. Look at your site, estimate both the expected traffic (i.e., number of users) and the amount of data each user will need to receive (based on how graphic-intensive or large your site's pages are), and try to negotiate a fixed *minimum guaranteed* bandwidth level which will always be available to your site, with required reporting and progressively steep penalties if the hosting company fails to live up to its obligations. Negotiating such a guarantee obligates your host company to give your customers access.

Managing Technical Difficulties

ALL THE GUARANTEED BANDWIDTH IN THE WORLD, THOUGH, will not help you if the server or connection is down with technical problems. This is generally addressed through uptime guarantees. No computer system is foolproof, or maintenance-free, and some problems will not be preventable by the hosting company, regardless of its efforts. Nor is it reasonable to expect the hosting firm to promise interruption-free service. However, it is important to get some high level of guaranteed hardware and network uptime into the contract (excluding a small amount of scheduled maintenance, to be performed during the projected slow time for your site, if possible), with discounts or rebates for failure to meet those guarantees.

In addition to the uptime standards, the hosting company should spell out how it will be notified when a problem does arise, how soon after that notification it will inform your company, and what steps it will take to minimize the duration and consequences of any service outage or hardware failure. The hosting company should also be encouraged to negotiate its own guarantees with the "upstream" bandwidth provider which supplies its Internet connections.

SERVER SECURITY

ANOTHER AREA THAT SHOULD BE CAREFULLY DISCUSSED WITH your hosting provider is server security, both physical and electronic. Keep in mind that your goal in outsourcing any service, such as the hosting of your Web site, is having the outsourcer take at least as much care with the company's equipment and information as you would. Since the actual management of the facility is out of your company's control, your contract must obligate the hosting firm to perform the necessary tasks and continue appropriate vigilance.

Physical security refers to access to the buildings that house the computers and lines through which the site is hosted. The hosting company should limit access to those areas to necessary personnel only, whether through human guards, passkeys, alarms, or some combination of those methods. The hosting firm should give authorized personnel of your company the ability to access the facility at any hour, either by themselves or (if the company has responsibility for hardware or software maintenance) with technicians. If this provision is breached, the hosting company should be liable for all damages caused by anyone other than your employees or contractors. Don't forget to periodically inspect the facility as well, to verify the hosting company's claims of security measures and assess whether the measures appear sufficient.

Electronic protection is the other critical part of any hosting arrangement. The operating systems and connection protocols used for Internet hosting are not entirely bug-free or secure. There are some commonly known "holes" in most systems. There are also well-publicized methods for closing those holes, and you should be sure that your hosting company is aware of and promptly implements them. Make sure it stays in contact with CERT, the Computer Emergency Response Team (the industry-sponsored independent body responsible for virus and security alerts), whose Web site is found at <http://www.cert.org>. It also may be a good idea for you to hire an independent computer security expert to audit the hosting company's precautions or even attempt an electronic incursion to test their effectiveness. At the same time, make sure to arrange electronic access to the site for your authorized personnel as well, to facilitate maintenance and updates of the content.

CONFIDENTIALITY

CONFIDENTIALITY PERTAINS TO THE SECURITY OF THE INFORmation within the site, as well as the user data (including credit card numbers) which may be transmitted by your customers. Keep in mind that the hosting company, by virtue of its administration of the server computers, probably has access to every piece of data passing through its systems. Make sure that it enforces a corporate policy of respecting and protecting data, and back up that policy with stringent contractual confidentiality obligations similar to those discussed in "Building Your Web Site." If you have committed to a specific level of user privacy by means of a published policy, which we'll explore in Chapter 2, the hosting company must also abide by the policy. Be sure to get a written acknowledgment in the contract of your company's ownership of the data transmitted to the site. You may also wish to verify that you will not be sharing a host server with any of your competitors, where the opportunity and temptation to intercept your proprietary information might be greater.

Coming to the End of the Line— Terminating a Hosting Relationship

IT'S IMPORTANT TO LOOK FORWARD TO THE END OF THE hosting relationship, just as it is with a developer, when crafting a risk-sensitive contract. Remember that the hosting firm has physical and electronic control over the materials and information of your site. What happens when you want to terminate the relationship, for cost or convenience, or because the hosting company has failed to meet its obligations? In the worst-case scenario, the hosting company locks you out of the computer on which your site is stored, both physically and electronically, and requires you to pay a "ransom" or to settle outstanding claims on less-than-equitable terms before returning it to you.

Although there is no absolute way to prevent this, there are a number of steps, both contractual and practical, which you can take to minimize the risk and increase the chance that, if this does occur, it will not inconvenience you. First, try to keep a current or all-but-current version of your site mirrored at another location, preferably on an internal computer at your company. This can be done by retaining a copy of everything you give to this hosting company. If you will not be directly providing the materials (or if your site includes outside input such as chat and user transactions), you can require the hosting company to periodically compress all the materials from your site and provide them to you via e-mail or on a disk or tape in an agreed-upon format. Make sure the contract itself provides a mechanism and a process for relocating your site to a server that you specify following termination of the agreement. The hosting firm should be obligated to cooperate with you and assist you in moving the site, although you may be required to pay any of its out-of-pocket costs for this service. Finally, make sure you have technically sophisticated people available to you (either on staff or via subcontract) who understand how hosting works and who can help you create the infrastructure to support your site should you need to quickly relocate it.

Disaster Recovery

DISASTER RECOVERY IS IMPORTANT IN TERMS OF BOTH GOOD business planning and risk assessment and management. Computers and Internet routers are fragile machines, prone to malfunction or damage, and even secure hosting facilities can be rendered inoperative through natural disaster, fire, or power outage. When investigating and contracting with hosting companies, determine what procedures and equipment the host has in place to prevent and address disasters that could shut down your site. In some cases, the hosting company may operate "mirrored" locations to improve speed.

In other situations, the hosting company may not neces-

Less@ Risk: Who's the Safest One of All? Mirroring a Site

IN A MIRRORING ENVIRONMENT, each hosted site is duplicated on a number of different servers across the country or the world, spreading out the requests from users to a manageable level. Besides improving general site performance, mirroring is a great way to manage shutdowns of one location due to disaster, since (if properly configured) the other locations can immediately and transparently "pick up the slack," assuming all the mirrors are current.

sarily operate real-time mirrors, but may have arrangements with a disaster-recovery company to make regular backups of all critical files, which can replace the live site and provide public access if the host's location is shut down. The hosting company should have equipment or procedures at its own facility to minimize the risk of shutdowns, such as:

◆ redundant connectivity to the Internet, usually through multiple backbone providers
◆ backup power generators with sufficient capacity to handle extended outages
◆ RAID (redundant array of inexpensive drives) or other technology for quickly substituting for failed hard drives
◆ automated fire-suppression systems, preferably based on halon or other methods which will not short out the surrounding computers

Usually, you can ask to see these procedures in writing prior to contract negotiations. Then, remember to specify the agreed-upon disaster recovery options and plans in the hosting agreement to ensure that the company is at least contractually obligated to maintain the level of vigilance and caution throughout the term of the relationship that it had at the outset.

At best, the hosting company will become your partner in easing the connection of your business to the Internet and the world. In the end, the quality of the service you receive from your hosting company will depend not only on the technical wizardry of the service's employees, but its sophistication and dedication to quality service and risk management. Making a Web site available to the public on a real-time basis is a complicated process, with many different products and services working in tandem. The hosting firm's failure to understand what could go wrong and to provide reasonable solutions to these potential problems should be your clue to find another company that would be sensitive to the stability and reliability of your Web site.

SAMPLE CONTRACT PROVISIONS— WEB SITE HOSTING AGREEMENTS
Bandwidth Guarantee Provision

◆ **Bandwidth.** In exchange for the payment of the monthly hosting fee, BarBYou shall be entitled to use no more than 1Mbps of a fractional T1 connection to which its server computer shall be attached (the "Fractional T1"). Notwithstanding the foregoing, Hosting Company shall provide no less than 512Kbps at all times of bandwidth from the Fractional T1 to BarBYou's server computer (the "Minimum Guaranteed Bandwidth"). If at any time Hosting Company shall fail to provide such Minimum Guaranteed Bandwidth during any given calendar month, BarBYou shall receive a credit against the following month's hosting fees equal to $____ for each aggregate hour or portion thereof for which the Minimum Guaranteed Bandwidth shall not be provided to BarBYou's server, up to a maximum credit of $____. If BarBYou shall fail to receive Minimum Guaranteed Bandwidth for more than ____ aggregate hours in each of two consecutive months, such failure shall be deemed a material breach of this Agreement by Hosting Company, entitling BarBYou to exercise its termination rights under §____ hereof, in addition to any other remedies to which BarBYou may be entitled.

Termination Provision

◆ **Termination.** Upon termination of this Agreement for any reason, Hosting Company will provide reasonable cooperation to BarBYou upon written request from BarBYou to enable BarBYou to relocate the Site to its own computer or another computer specified by it. Such cooperation may include, but is not limited to, providing complete copies of all then-current files comprising the Site on CD-R to BarBYou; providing a detailed run book with step-by-step instructions on operating and maintaining the Site; notifying InterNIC or other relevant DNS service of the change in the Site's IP address following the transition; and providing reasonable access to BarBYou and/or its contractors to facilitate the changeover. Except in the case of termination due to uncured material breach by Hosting Company, wherein Hosting Company shall bear all costs of such cooperation, Hosting Company shall not be obligated to incur any out-of-pocket costs (other than regular staffing costs) due to its cooperation at termination as provided in this paragraph.

CONTENT-ING YOURSELF

IN DISCUSSIONS ABOUT A WEB SITE, YOU WILL OFTEN HEAR the word *content* without much explanation, and many people misunderstand its meaning. Content refers not to the programming that makes the site function but to those elements of a Web site that are viewed or heard by the users:

◆ text
◆ graphics
◆ photos
◆ music
◆ audio and video recording
◆ animation

For most business sites, the content will come from the company's own materials, from a creative agency hired to fill the site with original or reused elements, or a combination of the two.

Content creation begins with the question, "What is our site going to be all about?" If your intention is primarily to save on customer support costs and to improve the quality of your responses, a site heavy in product and service information is the best choice. Public companies often also post press releases and annual or quarterly reports, fulfilling their mandate to provide information to current and prospective shareholders. Government agencies now publish reports, announcements, forms, and archived files online to save money on printing costs.

If the primary reason for the site is brand building, you may put up advertising copy, a contest or other prize promotion, coupons that can be printed, or your corporate history. Some sites are devoted to building community and include chat areas or tips and techniques for a particular interest group. Many Web sites have multiple goals. One advantage of a Web site, as opposed to print or broadcasting, is that there's little price premium on adding more and more content, so many companies will put just about everything on their Web sites, providing a coherent and consistent navigation system across the different sections.

There are numerous aids for choosing and designing good content, from books to Web sites to consultants and advertising agencies. The best way to select partners or references for your Web site is to turn to the same kinds of resources that you have used in the past. For most companies, it makes much more sense to carry over the existing corporate image and culture than to diverge sharply from what has gone before. Such divergence makes it more difficult to evaluate the success of the Web site, since you'll have to figure out whether the new image or some other aspect of the site, such as the technology, was responsible for the result. It also treats the Web site as somehow different from the core of the business rather than more properly as a powerful extension of your company. At the same time, though, make sure that your resources understand both the features and limitations of the Web as a medium. Otherwise, you run the chance of building a site that is too frustrating or too inaccessible for your targeted audience.

Content creation and publishing carry a variety of risks, combining very diverse areas of law and regulation. Later sections will address questions about specific kinds of content, from running a contest to providing a list of links, but all content shares certain similarities when it comes to risk strategies. The first question to ask when deciding on content for your site is, "Do we have the right to utilize these materials for international digital transmission?" The answer depends on any number of factors, but the major legal ones are:

◆ Copyright and trademark
◆ Talent issues and rights of privacy and publicity
◆ Content-specific prohibitions in the law

The most familiar of these categories is that of copyright and trademark. Often confused, they are in fact very different ways of providing legal protection to words or images, and the differences are important.

Copyright—an Original Source of ©onfusion

COPYRIGHT IS THE NAME FOR THE COLLECTION OF RIGHTS held under U.S. and most international law by the creator of an artistic or literary work (including computer software and audio recordings). Copyright allows the creator to limit or direct how a work is used, copied, modified, broadcast, or performed.

Under most countries' laws, copyright protection happens the moment a work is created, without any requirement to file with a government office or even put a copyright "notice" (such as "© 1997 John Q. Public") on the work. (The filing and notice may be required prior to suing for infringement, or may yield greater damages being won by the copyright holder if an infringement is found.) Under U.S. law, the copyright in most employees' works is automatically owned by their employer as a "work made for hire"—this is *not* the case for an independent contractor, who needs to transfer rights in writing, as we saw earlier in this chapter.

Because copyright protection is automatic, and because almost everything making up the content of a site is subject to copyright protection, you and those assisting you *must* take note of copyright obligations when creating a Web site for your business. If you're using a third-party developer, follow the guidelines outlined earlier in "Building Your Web

Creator's List of Rights, from the U.S. Copyright Law

(17 U.S.C. §106)
SUBJECT TO SECTIONS 107 THROUGH 120, the owner of copyright under this title has the exclusive rights to do and to authorize any of the following:

(1) to reproduce the copyrighted work in copies or phono-records;

(2) to prepare derivative works based upon the copyrighted work;

(3) to distribute copies or phonorecords of the copyrighted work to the public by sale or other transfer of owner-ship, or by rental, lease, or lending;

(4) in the case of literary, musical, dramatic, and choreo-graphic works, pantomimes, and motion pictures and other audiovisual works, to perform the copyrighted work publicly;

(5) in the case of literary, musical, dramatic, and choreo-graphic works, pantomimes, and pictorial, graphic, or sculptural works, including the individual images of a motion picture or other audiovisual work, to display the copyrighted work publicly; and

(6) in the case of sound recordings, to perform the copy-righted work publicly by means of a digital audio trans-mission.

Site" for acquiring rights from the developer and from any third parties whose materials are included in your site. If any of the materials going into your site are provided by your company, review the agreements (if any) under which you originally obtained them. Even if you paid for a full buyout, there may be restrictions on the media, geographic scope, and time frame for the buyout. Often you may have pur-chased a buyout for television or print use, which does not cover Internet distribution—if it doesn't say it in writing, you haven't received those rights from the creator, and shouldn't use it on your site. You should also be careful to verify that materials you believe to be created in-house actually were, and that the employees who created them did not simply modify existing copyrighted materials in inappropriate ways.

MYTHS ABOUT COPYRIGHT

AS EASY AS IT IS TO OBTAIN COPYRIGHT PROTECTION FOR A literary or artistic work, it's at least as easy to infringe on someone else's copyright, often without realizing it. Unfortunately, there are a number of commonly held myths about copyright and its limitations. If your employees believe any of the following myths, you may include unauthorized work within your Web site without meaning to, so it's important to educate your creative and technical personnel about these misconceptions:

◆ **Myth 1: Changing a certain percentage of an image removes its copyright protection.** NO—a copyright holder holds the same rights in "derivative works" as he or she does in the original work. No amount of change removes copyright protection.

◆ **Myth 2: Publicly accessible means freely usable.** NO— you must check the source of copyrighted materials before using them, even if they are easily obtained or without apparent protection. For example, even "freeware" software, which may be used and copied without payment, is subject to copyright, and the accompanying license may restrict use. Free availability is quite different from public domain, where no copyright applies.

◆ **Myth 3: Having a license to use materials for traditional media grants an automatic Web site usage license.** NO—each medium may require separate clearance and/or payment. That means that you may not have the right to put your award-winning TV commercial on your site.

◆ **Myth 4: The "Fair Use" exception to copyright allows unlimited use of materials if there is no admission or viewing fee for the use of the site.** NO—the fair use exception, whose categories are set by the courts rather than by federal law, is very limited, generally applying only to excerpts and then only for newsworthy, educational, not-for-profit, satirical, or similar uses. You can never be certain ahead of time whether a use would be considered fair use: the more of a work you use, the closer to commercial the use, or the greater the distribution, the less likely that you will be allowed a fair use defense to an infringement action.

If you are not careful about monitoring the source and rights for the materials included within your Web site, you may get sued for infringement. Because the scope of the prohibited activity is relevant to the award of damages, an infringement on the Internet, with its worldwide reach to millions, can be particularly expensive for the infringing party. It's also fairly easy for a copyright owner to discover whether its works are being used online. Search engines allow a copyright holder to seek out uses of a work by name, text, or description. If a lawsuit is brought and an infringement has occurred, the owner of the site on which the infringing material is placed can at best hope for a settlement with some sort of license fee being paid, and at worst, a judgment with the cost and negative publicity which accompanies it.

Trademark—Establishing a Brand Identity

TRADEMARK LAW IS MARKEDLY DIFFERENT FROM COPYRIGHT, not only in what it protects but how and for how long. Trademark refers to words, images, and other works used to identify the *source of goods and/or services in commerce*. A few important points to note:

◆ A corporate name may be, but is not necessarily, the same as a trademark. For example, "Xerox" is a U.S. registered trademark of the Xerox Corporation, indicated by the ® symbol.

◆ Use "in commerce" is specifically defined by the Patent and Trademark Office. In order to obtain registration of a mark, you have to show that it was displayed to the consumer in the course of a commercial transaction, not just printed in a press release.

◆ Although copyright law in the United States and elsewhere protects a work automatically upon creation, U.S. trademark law requires that a mark actually be used in commerce and that a request for registration be filed with the Patent and Trademark Office before registration will be issued. The use requirement prevents companies from "banking" long lists of marks to keep competitors from ever using them. Under current procedure, though, you may file an "intent to use" application to start the process, converting to a full application with evidence of use prior to getting registration. Additionally, if the registrant stops using the mark later, or fails to file renewals at the required times, the registration may lapse and others may use the mark.

◆ Since trademarks are used in commerce, the underlying principle is *avoiding consumer confusion*. Therefore, while registration of a mark will prohibit competing companies from using the mark, others in different fields may adopt the mark, as long as the consumer can tell the difference between the users (e.g., United Airlines and United Van Lines).

◆ While virtually all original library or artistic works are copyrightable, many words are not registrable as trademarks. For example, generic or merely descriptive terms may not be protected. An Italian restaurant cannot use trademark law to prevent its competitors from using the word *Pizzeria*, since it's a generic term for that industry, although a Web site design firm could register "Web Pizzeria" as a fanciful mark.

◆ Copyright holders have a much lower ongoing burden than do trademark registrants—once a copyright is established, it remains in existence throughout the entire statutory term. Not only can trademarks expire, but trademark owners must always be on the lookout for others infringing on their marks and are obligated to take action to halt any discovered infringement. Failure to affirmatively enforce a registered trademark can actually lead to loss of the mark.

◆ The holder of a popular trademark may become a victim of its own marketplace success: a trademark that enters the general lexicon to describe the whole class of goods or services could actually become generic and lose its protection. It happened to formerly-registered marks such as *Aspirin* and *Escalator*. Xerox Corporation now spends a large amount of money each year to remind consumers and journalists (by advertisement and cease and desist letter alike) that *Xerox* is

Xerox's Trademark Statement

THE XEROX TRADEMARK. Xerox is a well-known trademark and trade name. Xerox as a trademark is properly used only as a brand name to identify the company's products and services. The Xerox trademark should be used as a proper adjective followed by the generic name of the product: Xerox copier/Xerox printer. The Xerox trademark should not be used as a verb. The trade name Xerox stands for the full corporate name: Xerox Corporation.

<http://www.xerox.com/go/xrx/about_xerox/about_xerox_detail.jsp?view=factbook&id=11170&sub=2> (April 25, 1999)

a proper noun, meaning one doesn't "xerox" something or use a "xerox machine."

Unfortunately, establishing and protecting trademarks on the Web is not nearly as simple as with copyright. To begin with, although there is some reciprocity among different countries' trademark registries, there are no international trademark standards or laws. Individual countries or even states have their own requirements and limitations. By placing your site on the Web from the United States, you may be deemed to be infringing the trademark of a similarly named company in Germany, which could adversely affect any present or future operations you have in that country. Similarly, your customers might be confused by a foreign-based Web site using similar marks to yours and perhaps even selling the same products.

The potential for confusion is even stronger when questions of domain names enter the trademark picture. A domain name is the text version of the IP (Internet Protocol) numerical addresses that are assigned to every computer hooked up to the Internet. Domain names are useful because they are much easier to remember than IP addresses, just as telephone numbers like 800-MATTRES are simpler to recall than their numerical equivalents. IP addresses take the form of four sets of three-digit numbers, separated by dots—for example, the IP address for the main Bloomberg Web site is 204.179.240.180; the domain name is <http://www.bloomberg.com>. Unfortunately, domain names do a mediocre job at best of promoting and utilizing trademarks, because they are much more limited than trademarks:

◆ Trademarks can be letters, numbers, words, sentences, special characters, graphics, photos, sound, music, even a color. Domain names are limited to the letters A-Z, the numbers 0-9, and a hyphen. This means that there are many more potential trademarks than domain names, and only a limited number of trademarks will have exact domain name equivalents.

◆ Although many different companies in different industries can share a single mark, only a single registrant can have each domain name within a given "top-level domain" (such as .com, .org, or country codes like .co.uk for commercial sites within the United Kingdom). For example, "Kraft.com" was first registered by Kraft Foods way back on February 11, 1995. Any other company which uses the word "Kraft" for its trademark would have to find another domain name, one which was likely to be less obvious. Because each country can operate its own domain name service, accessible throughout the Internet, companies with worldwide trademarks have a choice of either registering in every possible country or allowing foreign companies to usurp their marks with local domain names. While Apple Computer owns "Apple.com" and many other international domain names beginning with "Apple," a Web artist agency called The Apple Agency Ltd. owns "Apple.co.UK," even though Apple Computer markets to U.K. customers.

◆ Those who infringe registered trademarks can be fought in court with clear statutory authority on the part of the registered mark owner. Improper use of domain names, on the other hand, may be disputed only via the policies of the private registries which issue them, policies which may or may not be consistent with applicable trademark law.

Ultimately, if you wish to encourage traffic to your Web site, you cannot depend on a trademark-derived domain name alone to bring people to you, since the domain name system will do an increasingly poor job as an identifying mechanism as more sites come online. Rather, utilize a smart "cyberPR" strategy, combining targeted submission and keyword purchases on the most popular search engines and indices, banner and other advertising buys at Web sites also frequented by your target audience, and link sharing and similar arrangements to make your site more easily clickable. Also consider choosing a domain name which, while not the same as your trademark, is still distinctive. For example, if you have an easily remembered telephone number, choose a domain name to match it (for example, if your number is 800-555-5000, you could register 555-5000.com as your domain name).

You should also get into the habit of using the tools commonly available on the Internet to verify and enforce proper use of your business's existing trademarks. It's a matter of a few minutes to put your company's name and popular trademarks into a search engine such as Altavista <http://www.altavista.com> or Hotbot <http://www.hotbot.com>. What you find may startle you. Beyond the obvious uses (for example, if you distribute goods to retailers, the retailers' sites may utilize your marks to sell the goods), you may discover that your competitors' sites come up in a search for your mark, even if you cannot see the mark used on the suspect Web page. There are a number of Web site development and formatting tricks, from so-called *white text* (white lettering, invisible to the user, placed on white background) to Meta tag bombing (nondisplaying information included under the <meta> HTML tag), which are specifically designed to catch, and fool, automated search engines. While the search engine companies attempt to filter out inappropriate and misleading sites from their lists, savvy marketers have managed to stay one step ahead of the technology and continue to intentionally mislead Web surfers to their sites. If you do discover an inappropriate use of your trademark, keep in mind that, just as if the use were in print or broadcast media, inappropriate trademark use on the Internet by a third party may well be grounds for an infringement action or, at the least, a strongly worded cease and desist letter from your lawyers.

What Is Usenet?

USENET NEWS GROUPS are one of the older applications on the Internet, well predating the development of the Web in the early 1990s. In the Usenet system, messages on thousands of different topics from individual users are automatically sorted and distributed across the Internet by specialized software. Readers can choose which of the topics they wish to follow, and can read messages sorted by subtopic. Usenet news groups run the gamut from dry discussions of computer technology (comp.protocols.dns, for example) to pet tips (rec.pets.cats.health) to more adult topics (alt.sex. stories). While Usenet messages are text-only, unlike the graphic-rich Web, techniques have been developed for turning binary files (such as software and images) into text temporarily for posting to Usenet. This technique is probably most frequently used in the news groups where people post pornographic images scanned from magazines or videos, although it has practical business application as well.

A Web search for your mark isn't sufficient, though. The Internet is made up of a number of different kinds of information-publishing methods: the Web is one, and so-called Usenet news groups are another.

The problem with Usenet from a business perspective is that anyone can post anything, without attribution or proof, and have the statement immediately distributed to literally millions of potential readers. Many companies' services have been criticized in a Usenet posting, either by legitimately unhappy customers or by competitors masquerading as customers. Luckily, Web sites such as Deja <http://www.Deja.com> archive Usenet postings and allow searching of their content. If your company is criticized on Usenet, you need to choose whether or not to reply, and if so, whether to do so publicly to the group or privately to the sender, in the hopes that the sender will post a follow-up message describing your fast and complete response to the problem.

Finally, remember that you should ensure you're not violating others' trademarks with the content of your site, in addition to protecting your own marks. Before you select and start publishing the name for a Web site, or for a prominent section within the site, do a complete trademark search. Performed by agencies such as Thomson & Thomson, these searches will tell you whether or not the names you have chosen or other similar ones, including domain names, are registered by competing companies within your industry. The few hundred dollars or more spent for such a search will prevent having to change marketing materials and site content and possibly defend against an infringement action.

Identifying Talent and Moral Right Problems

ALL THE COPYRIGHT AND TRADEMARK VIGILANCE AND LICENSing in the world will not guarantee you're in the clear for the photos and recordings you wish to use on your Web sites— you must also be aware of talent rights and related moral rights (or droits morals). Talent rights, a broad description of legal rights including the rights of privacy and publicity, essentially relate to the right of a person to control how his or her face, name, or voice is used for commercial purposes. Like trademark, talent rights vary by state and by country, and questions such as how long rights survive after the death of a celebrity differ sharply depending on the applicable jurisdiction.

Ordinary people depicted in photos or otherwise identifiable in materials to be posted to a Web site may protest or forbid their inclusion, or demand payment prior to permitting this use. Celebrities have a broader set of rights, and the courts have generally decided that while people in the public eye have less of a right to privacy, their corresponding right to publicity (that is, the control over how their identity is used for commercial purposes) may be greater than for noncelebrities, since it is their fame which provides the basis for their income. Celebrities have obtained court relief under their rights of privacy and publicity when a sound-alike was used for a musical commercial, or in one celebrated case involving *Wheel of Fortune's* Vanna White, where a robot in a blond wig was shown in a TV commercial turning letters.

An in-depth analysis of talent rights is beyond the scope of this book, and should be undertaken with experienced counsel for any major media project (whether a Web site or a print ad). Here, though, are a few important points about both copyright and talent rights to consider whenever materials you wish to use contain identifiable images or sounds of real people:

◆ When using stock photos or any other images or video with recognizable faces, the people depicted may have to give permission separately from the owner of the copyright. Make sure that the archive supplier has obtained from the talent releases covering Internet use, or that the archive will indemnify your company if you ever get sued by the talent for using the work.

◆ If rights for works have been negotiated in the past, expect difficulty and high costs to renegotiate any Internet rights not covered by the original buyout. Make it your company's policy to get the broadest possible rights for the longest term when negotiating for uses of copyrighted materials, particularly with identifiable talent. Also, try to cover any locality to whose laws your site or your company may be subject— ideally, get a worldwide license, covering "all media now in existence and hereinafter created, including but not limited to the Internet".

◆ If using recorded music, particularly with vocal tracks, on your Web site, there are many parties whose permissions you will need to obtain (and pay for). These include the publisher of the original composition, who may be compensated through ASCAP or BMI, two of the major music publisher organizations; the copyright holder of the actual recording, which may be the record company; and any recognizable voices and musicians on the recording. Many of these negotiations are covered by union and guild agreements, with which you must comply in order to use the materials. Similar agreements cover talent and music contained within video and film recordings.

- Even if the person depicted in a photo or video or sound clip is not immediately recognizable, the work itself may be sufficiently famous to generate publicity rights. For example, there is a famous photo of Edwin (Buzz) Aldrin standing on the moon, taken by Neil Armstrong (whose spacesuit is reflected in the opaque visor of Aldrin's helmet). While Aldrin's face is not visible through the helmet visor, the picture is world-famous and known to be of Aldrin. As a result, Aldrin enforces his rights of publicity over commercial uses of the photo, even though NASA owns the copyright.

- Internationally obtained materials add a further layer of complication, since well-known figures abroad may not be immediately recognizable to U.S. business owners. Nonetheless, placing the work on a Web site makes it accessible to such personalities, who may take action against the U.S. company and/or any foreign subsidiaries. Other concerns about non-U.S. Internet material is discussed below.

Whereas talent rights protect the name, face, or voice of a famous person, moral rights are meant to uphold something less tangible: reputation. The moral rights laws, which are quite strong in Europe (especially France) and growing in

Sample Waiver Language for U.S. Law

YOU AGREE THAT no advertisement or other material or use of the Art, including but not limited to the placement of the Art in materials to be made available via television commercials and/or on the World Wide Web of the Internet, need be submitted to you for any further approval, and BarBYou will be without liability to you for any distortion or illusionary effect resulting from use of the Art. In this regard, you hereby expressly waive any rights you may have regarding the Art pursuant to the Visual Artist Rights Act (17 U.S.C. §106A(e)).

popularity in the United States, allow an artist to claim authorship of a work and to protect the integrity of both name and style from alteration or misuse in a way which might harm the artist's reputation. In most cases, moral rights are separate from copyright, and more difficult (if not impossible) for the artist to give up or sell. U.S. copyright law contains limited moral rights protections in the so-called Visual Artist Rights Act, found at 17 U.S.C. §106A, and individual states have put such provisions into their laws as well. In the case of the U.S. law, the artist may waive his or her rights only expressly in writing, even if the author either never had or already sold or gave away the copyright to the work.

Once again, to the extent that work included in your Web site is known or suspected to come from outside the United States, the rules (and ability of the artist to waive moral rights) may sharply differ from the above U.S. law, and the same is true for copyright, trademark, and talent rights. Accordingly, it is crucial to work closely with a knowledgeable attorney before including any outside artistic or literary work in your Web site.

Navigating Content-Specific Laws

SURVIVING THE MINEFIELD OF COPYRIGHT, TRADEMARK, and related issues is only one aspect of reducing the legal risk arising out of your site's content. Depending on what kind of site you are building, there may be laws and regulations specifically focused on the type of material you are posting on the Internet. Some examples of these laws include:

◆ Securities laws for public companies and investment-related information
◆ Mandatory disclosure required for certain industries, such as pharmaceutical sales
◆ Potential malpractice actions from users unduly relying on advice posted to the site
◆ Antitrust restrictions on publishing pricing, soliciting collaboration, etc.

- Consumer protection and import/export laws for online retailing
- Age-restrictions and outright prohibitions for controversial Web sites focusing on gambling, sexually explicit materials, and other potentially criminal activity
- Truth-in-advertising and other marketing-related laws
- Privacy laws and restrictions on the use or redistribution of personally identifiable information
- Libel laws arising out of content posted by you, and even by third parties in chat areas or message boards enabled on your Web site
- Technology export restrictions for software, hardware designs, and other materials

Although this list is far from exhaustive, it is imposing enough. Many of the more common content liability concerns (such as online contests and advertising or link liability) will be dealt with in detail in subsequent sections. Here, though, is a checklist you can follow to evaluate and deal with the risks associated with selecting and publishing Web-based content:

AN ONLINE CONTENT CHECKLIST

- Think carefully about your choice of content—use only those elements that positively contribute to your Web site goals, and that load and display efficiently on the equipment owned by your likely target audience.
- Educate everyone involved in obtaining and manipulating content in basic legal concepts such as copyright and talent rights and about your risk management strategy.
- Determine, verify, and document the original source of all materials being placed on your Web site. Remember—just because you get something from a publisher or other Web site doesn't mean that it originated there or that your source had the right to pass it along to you.
- Don't make unnecessary work for yourself. If public domain materials (such as U.S. government-created works, which are not subject to copyright protection) can serve your purpose, don't use protected works. If you can avoid including recognizable talent or art within your site, do so.

- If any part of your site contains content contributed by a third party, make sure that such party knows of and remains responsible for content risk assessment, and back it up with your own periodic review.

- If your business has a procedure for reviewing traditional corporate communications, put your Web content through that process before it goes live on the Web. Repeat this for any updates you do to the site. Remember that material you publish on a Web site is immediately more broadly distributed than almost anything else your business can publish or broadcast.

- Include appropriate disclaimers within your site, and make them easy to find. This "legalese" should list the copyright and trademark owners in the site, let your users know for whom the site is intended, and what country's laws you intend to apply to the content and any disputes related to the site. Examples of these disclaimers can be gleaned from the larger commercial Web sites, usually via a link from the copyright notice at the bottom of a page.

- Establish a process by which someone experienced in content risk analysis continually reviews your site, and make sure that urgent changes can be done immediately to shield your company from liability. Chapter 4 gives advice on finding qualified professional advisers.

Above all, keep in mind that beyond the technology that makes your site run, the content provides its identity, brand distinctiveness, and appeal to users. Unfortunately, improperly or negligently included content within a site can produce significant legal vulnerability to you and your business. Appropriate caution and procedures, though, go far to prevent content hazards.

SAMPLES FROM U.S. COPYRIGHT LAW

TO UNDERSTAND COPYRIGHT, YOU NEED TO LOOK TO THE source, in this case the Copyright Act. From 17 U.S.C. § 101: Definitions:

A "work made for hire" is—

1 a work prepared by an employee within the scope of his or her employment; or

2 a work specially ordered or commissioned for use as a contribution to a collective work, as a part of a motion picture or other audiovisual work, as a translation, as a supplementary work, as a compilation, as an instructional text, as a test, as answer material for a test, or as an atlas, if the parties expressly agree in a written instrument signed by them that the work shall be considered a work made for hire....

More on the question of ownership and control can be found in this excerpt from 17 U.S.C. § 201, entitled "Ownership of copyright":

(a) Initial Ownership.—Copyright in a work protected under this title vests initially in the author or authors of the work. The authors of a joint work are co-owners of copyright in the work.

(b) Works Made for Hire.—In the case of a work made for hire, the employer or other person for whom the work was prepared is considered the author for purposes of this title, and, unless the parties have expressly agreed otherwise in a written instrument signed by them, owns all of the rights comprised in the copyright.

(c) Contributions to Collective Works.—Copyright in each separate contribution to a collective work is distinct from copyright in the collective work as a whole, and vests initially in the author of the contribution. In the absence of an express transfer of the copyright or of any rights under it, the owner of copyright in the collective work is presumed to have acquired only the privilege of reproducing and distributing the contribution as part of that particular collective work, any revision of that collective work, and any later collective work in the same series.

SAMPLE RELEASE PROVISION FOR WEB SITE ART

By signing this agreement, you give and grant to BarBYou for a period of _____ a nonexclusive license to use the Art in all media and types of advertising and promotion of BarBYou, including but not limited to in advertising and promotion in television commercials and/or utilizing the Internet's World Wide Web. Permitted users include BarBYou, its affiliates, and its and their employees, agents, and independent contractors. BarBYou shall have the unlimited worldwide right to exploit the Art as it sees fit, including the right to alter or rearrange the Art.

GETTING STARTED IN E-COMMERCE

INTERNET RETAILING IS AN EXCITING WAY TO LAUNCH YOUR business online. Unlike the sponsorship model, which requires an investment of time and money in a Web site to generate traffic and profitable advertising sales, online retailing brings in direct revenue, with easily calculated profit margins on each sale. Electronic commerce (*e-commerce*, sometimes called *e-business*) is also the most familiar way for traditional businesses to use the Internet, particularly those companies already involved in catalog retailing.

Virtual Retail

CONTRAST PREPARING A WEB SITE WITH OPENING AN ACTUAL store in a shopping district of a city or town. Outside of the cost of the space and fixtures, there may be zoning and signage restrictions, business licenses, staffing issues, neighborhood shifts, worries about crime rates, and the possibility that a street closing due to a water main break or construction accident could prevent customers from ever reaching your door. In most cities, even if you don't want to go through the trouble of opening a full store, you can't just set up a table on the street and hock your wares. A police officer will quickly write you a citation for unlicensed peddling, and a strong gust of wind can turn your inventory into unidentified flying objects.

Catalog businesses are easier, but you need to choose printers and paper stock, buy mailing lists, figure postage, sort by area for bulk rate discounts, send out the catalogs, and worry that they will be ruined by bad weather or turned into bird-cage liner.

A direct link to customers, less infrastructure and overhead, and a growing Internet user base are a few of the notable benefits of online retailing. Amazon.com (among the most famous of the online-only retailers) was a start-up in July 1995, a public company in May 1997, and reporting sales in second quarter 1998 of $116 million! Other retailers from the auction site Onsale.com <http://www.onsale.com> to hot-sauce vendor Hothothot.com <http://www.hothothot.com> to travel and financial discounter Priceline <http://www.price-line.com> have made names and markets from online operations. And beyond the few marketers with national advertising budgets and large-scale financing, there are literally hundreds of thousands of individuals and companies all over the world selling new and used products online. It is almost as if everyone in the world was given a pushcart and allowed to stand on a street corner hawking wares.

For consumers, this incredible growth of online retailing also contains a number of significant benefits. Of primary importance is pricing—as more retailers reduce their overhead by being online-only operations, they can pass the cost savings on to consumers in the form of lower prices on the same goods. It goes beyond cost benefits, though; the same Web browser that brings the consumer to your shopping site can also link her to the product manufacturer's Web site for detailed specifications, to a consumer information site for test results and comparisons with other products, and to a chat room where past buyers of the product can discuss their experiences. A few clicks of the "back" button, and the newly informed customer may be ready to purchase. Once the customer makes her purchase, she may receive a shipping tracking number automatically via e-mail to enable her to know to the day when her package will arrive and a customer service I.D. number to enable more efficient after-purchase support. (In some cases, your shipping company may have custom tools to ease this process that work with specific Web development and server programs. You may wish to check this out before selecting a development environment for your site.)

Of course, establishing an online retail presence is not simple even for a traditional retailer. The challenges are sizable. This section will introduce you to some of the major risks to focus on in order to establish a successful online retail presence:

◆ Special site design, hosting, and software requirements
◆ Encryption and security
◆ Payment authorization
◆ Sales tax concerns

Building a Retailing Web Site

JUST AS BUILDING A STORE ON MAIN STREET HAS DIFFERENT requirements than constructing a house around the corner, building a retailing Web site has some unique considerations beyond the general elements outlined earlier in this chapter. The online retailing process remains simple for the customer although a complex series of communications are going on behind the scenes. For the user, the ideal online shopping trip involves finding a desired product in stock, selecting it, going to the checkout screen, putting in shipping and billing information in a secure environment, and confirming the purchase.

The machinations that must take place seamlessly in order for that simple customer transaction to occur are astonishing. Here is the same process, interwoven with the back-office elements supporting it:

1 **Customer finds a desired product in stock**
   a) Navigation and search commands connect to database of products to enable customer to find products
   b) Matching images and description of products provided from database (or fixed page, for simpler catalog)
2 **Customer selects product for purchase**
   a) Customer provided with button to place order or to put item in "shopping cart"
   b) If using shopping cart, user must be identified specifically,

items chosen listed either on the user's machine or on the server

c) New items must be added to any previously selected items in user's cart

3 Customer indicates a desire to check out

a) Any items from shopping cart must be designated for purchase so they will not be sold to other customers, listed with current pricing and shipping information, retrieved, and assigned to customer

b) Updated stock searches, either to a local warehouse or (for those companies with "virtual inventory") to supplier or distributor ensure all items in shopping cart are still available for immediate purchase

c) If not already in shopping cart, item is so designated

4 Customer puts in shipping and billing information

a) Form with appropriate blanks must be generated, placed on customer's screen

b) If encryption is available to protect security of customer's credit card information, it should be turned on at both browser and server and synchronized

c) Information must be monitored as entered, and compared to acceptable responses (e.g., no missing required fields, credit card data matches card defaults and number of digits; in some cases, addresses can be quickly verified against credit card records for an extra level of security for the vendor)

d) If shipping and billing addresses are different, customer should be queried to ensure this is intended

5 Customer confirms the purchase

a) Applicable shipping and tax must be calculated and added to total amount being charged to customer

b) All items to be purchased must be retrieved and displayed for final confirmation

c) If possible, shipping time frame must be calculated and displayed to customer

d) Customer's confirmation must be verified as coming from the same computer that placed the original order

e) Once order is confirmed, warehouse and shipping department need to be contacted to pack and ship the order

f) Following shipping, tracking information must be matched to customer data to enable both company and customer to track delivery

g) Once inventory is depleted, orders to replenish the warehouse must go to suppliers

h) Alternatively, for businesses that do not maintain their own warehouses, the confirmation of the order must pass from the retailer to its suppliers or distributors, who will be responsible for fulfilling the order in the name of the retailer and replenishing its own supplies of merchandise following shipment of orders.

At its heart, this process is not substantively different from that which occurs in any retail environment, from the smallest street vendor to the largest multinational mall anchor store. The difference, though, is that the entire process is (or should be) automated. Only the customer is human; almost every other aspect is handled by technology. Much of this technology is implemented at the level of the Web site and Web server, which will usually communicate with the customer's browser, the financial institution providing card clearance, the warehouse or supplier, the shipping company, and the customer again via e-mail. Fortunately, the prevalence of Internet technologies means that this communication can occur without the proprietary software and hardware previously needed to set up an online retail system.

It is crucial to choose a Web developer and hosting company for an online retail project that provide reliability, 24/7 connectivity, and security. The developer should be able to recommend appropriate tools that contain the back-office capability you need, or to suggest vendors to whom you can outsource the order processing. The latter involves building a site operated by the outsourcing company resembling your company's regular site. The outsourcer will provide you with access to all necessary software and payment clearance services, and pass orders through to you as you direct. The advantage for you, besides simply avoiding having to create an online payment and shipping infrastructure yourself, is that the vendor, by virtue of economies of scale, may affordably offer you a much more advanced and feature-rich retail environment.

If you choose the outsourcing route, test-drive some of the vendor's other sites, including making small purchases, to verify that the customer experience is as rapid and complete as if the order were going directly to the retailer itself. Similarly, try out some of the developer's own retail sites for usability and reliability, and make anonymous customer service calls to check whether the proper information has been passed on to the retailer and is accessible in the case of problems.

The hosting company should be questioned about:

◆ Reliability. This is particularly important when a customer could be interrupted in the midst of a purchase, and not know whether the order had gone through or not, leading to loss of confidence in the vendor.

◆ Number of companies or stores sharing the particular server or Internet connection (with options from having everything dedicated to partial to total sharing)

◆ Number of simultaneous transactions possible

◆ Confidentiality (since all purchasers will be providing financial and personal information as part of the transaction, and privacy breaches will yield tremendous loss of goodwill)

◆ Verification that pricing makes sense for your predicted margins. For example, a storefront priced on the number of items available rather than on a percentage or number of sales may be beneficial for a store featuring a small number of low-margin and/or low-cost items, whereas a vendor featuring high-margin items may be able to better afford a small per-transaction commission.

Most of all, be sure you can detail the required elements, even if not listing all companies who will participate in it, before you begin designing your site. The last thing you want is to invest in a design and server solution with which your critical supplier or delivery company is not compatible. It may be useful to hire an online retailing specialist to guide you through the process of selecting appropriate software and server choices for your sales goals, and to serve as your liaison to the technical contractors or internal personnel charged with creating your online retailing site.

Encryption and Security

SURVEY AFTER SURVEY OF ONLINE USERS SHOWS INCREDIBLE growth of the Internet, whether in homes, schools, or businesses. The growth of online retailing, though, has lagged behind the rest of the Internet. There are a number of reasons for this lag, but one of the major ones is the perception by consumers that online shopping is somehow less safe than the same purchase made in person or over the telephone.

For the most part, this perception is faulty. Even without encryption, electronic shopping represents one of the safest means of purchasing goods. As mentioned earlier, a message sent over the Internet is broken into many pieces called packets, each of which is sent on its own path, only to regroup as a single message at the destination. Even if someone can intercept some of the packets out of the many terabytes of information flowing across the Internet daily (1,099,511,627,776 bytes of information, or a thousand gigabytes, compared to 5 to 15 gigabytes of storage on a typical hard disk drive), it is not likely that the person would have enough of the message to recreate a credit card or social security number. It is much easier, and cheaper, for a would-be credit card thief to steal a receipt from a restaurant or store or pay someone to do so, lift a wallet from an unsuspecting person, or buy a credit card number from another thief.

Nevertheless, consumers continue to perceive Web-based commerce as unsecure, even when it is offered by well-known, traditional retailers. As a result, companies wishing to create online retail offerings must address not only the actual mechanics, but consumer fears as well. The best way to do this is with a combination of technology, primarily encryption technology, and clear explanations of what you are doing to safely collect and maintain your customers' financial information.

Encryption has been used for both military and business communications for literally millennia, from the earliest letter-for-letter replacement codes to the one-time-pad ciphers of espionage agents. The Internet version of encryption, though, is much more benign and easy to implement than those historical precedents, in part because one of the two parties (the consumer) need not do anything other than run a modern Web browser in order for reasonably secure encryption to work.

Web-based encryption relies on a protocol called SSL (for "Secure Sockets Layer"), originally implemented by Netscape Communications Corporation for its Navigator software. It is now part of most Web browser programs including Microsoft's Internet Explorer and the America Online browser. Most Web server programs (including Netscape Commerce Server, the shareware Apache server, and Microsoft's Internet Information Server) implement SSL as either a standard feature or a readily available add-on.

The public key/private key setup can be used in a number of ways to boost security and establish identities in cyberspace. For online commerce, the most common application is for the consumer to use the retailer's public key to encrypt and send credit card information—only the retailer, with its

The Secret of SSL

HOW DOES SSL PROTECT transmissions between customers and retailers? According to Netscape's Web site <http://developer.netscape.com/tech/security/ssl/howitworks.html>, Netscape uses a licensed technology called "Public Key Cryptography." In this method, each party to a communication maintains a private key that it alone knows (the browser software automatically generates this for the user). Based upon this private key, the party creates an unlimited number of public keys, which it provides to other parties. When a party wants to send a secure communication, it encrypts it using the other party's public key. Once the communication is encrypted with a public key, it can only be decrypted and read with the corresponding private key, so even the sending party can no longer read the message. By the same token, information encrypted with the *private* key can only be decrypted with the *public* key.

secret private key, can read the message and charge the card. In other situations, the sender can establish an identity definitively by encrypting a random message from the other party with the sender's private key, and returning the message to the other party. If the random message can be decoded with the sender's public key, the sender's identity is verified (a similar process is used to create so-called "digital signatures"). The mathematical relationship between the public and private keys is not fixed (although well-reported efforts have managed to crack software's private keys relatively quickly when the software's particular method for generating the public keys was discovered).

The level of security in public key encryption, like other encoding methods, is related to the size of the key, and is measured in "bits," essentially a power of two: in 40-bit encryption (the less-stringent type used in SSL), the number of possible keys is 2^{40}, or 1,099,511,627,776 (that's almost 1.1 trillion); 128-bit security provides 309,485,009,821,345,068,724,781,056 *times* that 1.1 trillion number of possible key combinations! 128-bit encryption is available from both Netscape and Microsoft, although its use has historically been limited by export restrictions placed on encryption technology by the U.S. government, which fears its use by terrorists and other criminals to foil intelligence-gathering activities by authorities. Under these regulations, Netscape and Microsoft have been able to make the 128-bit versions available to customers who can positively establish they are inside the United States—all other customers get the otherwise-identical 40-bit versions.

While current computing power can, under certain circumstances, crack 40-bit keys through so-called "brute force methods" in a matter of hours or days by combining many processors on specific algorithms, casual interception and decryption of 40-bit communications remain well beyond the capabilities of today's computers. Accordingly, 40-bit encryption is still "safe enough," particularly given the high volume of traffic on the Internet and the ease with which criminals can gather credit card numbers in other ways, but U.S. consumers can usually get the benefit of the more-secure 128-bit encryption with little or no additional cost.

Implementing SSL for your online store requires a number of steps. First, you must ensure that your server computer (or that of the hosting company you select) offers up-to-date versions of any of the SSL-compatible server software. If you are running the server yourself, you will need a Digital I.D. Certificate for the software, essentially the statement by a trusted third party that you are who you are—companies such as Verisign <http://www.verisign.com> issue them for a fee. At the same time, verify that all other known security holes have been plugged—it's no use offering encryption if a savvy criminal can electronically break into the machine and steal the information after it's been received. Don't forget that it's not just the electronic dangers that need to be addressed—physical security of the server and access to the data files must be strictly controlled as well, and any hosting company should promise such care in writing as part of the contract. For example, if you are not the only company to use and have access to the server computer, the hosting firm must demonstrate that the others sharing the machine cannot, and will not, be able to retrieve your customers' information or credit card numbers. The next step is to check that any data transmissions between your company and the transaction processing service you choose (see below) are at least as secure as that between you and your customers. Remember, even if your customers cannot always use 128-bit encryption because of export problems, if you and your transaction processing company are both in the United States, you should be able to establish 128-bit data transfer between you in all cases.

After the technical side is squared away, you come to the tricky part—assuring your customers that buying on the Internet is at least as safe as purchasing over the telephone. Explain to them in simple terms how the encryption works when they click on the "Check Out" button. Essentially, lead them through a sample purchase, from click to delivery, and show how your security is operating. (It's helpful to point out where on their particular browser they might see the encryption indicator.) You don't need to be overly technical, just factual, but make sure not to make promises about absolute security that could be legally binding on you in the event of a problem. If you'd like, you can also provide icons to vendor sites where they can download the latest secure versions of their favorite browser software.

Here are a few more suggestions to produce more confident (and willing) customers:

◆ For those consumers who are still not comfortable with online credit card transmission, even with your explanation, have a telephone and/or fax option available and clearly listed. It will be more costly for you to make those sales since you need to pay a live person to answer the phone or transcribe the fax, but perhaps less costly than lost sales.

◆ In order to reassure your buyers and deepen your relationship with them, follow up any purchases with confirming e-mail messages. Verify that you received the order, give them an order number for future queries, let them know the expected shipping date, even provide them with UPS/Federal Express tracking numbers and the address of the couriers' Web sites to track the delivery in real-time.

◆ In some cases, your hosting company may charge you extra for use of the secure server. It may be possible either to enable encryption only for the order-taking portion of the customer's Web session, or even to use two hosting companies, a cheaper one for the catalog and unsecure material, and a dedicated commerce server provider for the order processing. This should not interfere with your customers' experience, since they only go to the order portion of your site after they click on a button or link indicating their readiness to purchase. In order to manage a dual-server environment, format the page on the commerce server to look just like those on your regular site, and be *very* careful that all links and scripts properly return your customer to the original site upon completion of the transaction. Your customers should never even notice the transition, unless they happen to be looking at the address bar of their browsers when the switchover takes place. (For a helpful example of how this can work, and samples of vendors using this type of arrangement, you can refer to the Yahoo! Store site, formerly Viaweb, found at <http://store.yahoo.com>.)

Payment Authorization

CONSUMERS ARE ONE GROUP LEERY OF ONLINE COMMERCE.
Transaction processing companies are another. These businesses must deal with the risk of credit card fraud on the part of consumers in an environment in which their retail partners have scant information about the customers and, therefore, have little ability to judge customer credibility before a sale goes through. Nevertheless, a number of processing companies, from established players like Verifone (whose Web site at <http://www.verifone.com/solutions/internet/> discusses Internet payment options) to banks and small start-ups, are offering credit card and even check processing services to online retailers.

How do you distinguish among the many possible choices for transaction processing, and for what do you need to ask from a vendor? Consider these criteria when making your choice:

◆ **Cost.** As with shopping cart software, transaction processing firms have different compensation schemes based on volume, size of transactions, credit rating, likelihood (and history) of fraud, and whether a company is using the firm for other (offline) types of transaction processing. Don't be afraid to shop around and to negotiate better pricing.

◆ **Ease of integration.** Is the transaction processing system compatible with the shopping cart server you have selected? How about your banking and accounting systems? If not, how much work will it take to integrate the systems, and does the vendor have tools to assist in the process?

◆ **Reliability.** How reliable is the firm? After all, it is through its service that you will actually get paid for the goods you sell. Be sure not only to ask for references, but also to buy things anonymously through their clients' Web sites to see how smoothly the system works and whether the credit card charges you see are accurate and timely. You should also receive details and written guarantees of uptime and backup in the event the main processing facility is unavailable for service due to power or telecommunications outage or other causes.

◆ **Breadth of service.** What other services can the company offer you? Some transaction processing companies also provide consulting services, shopping cart software, smart-card and credit card readers for real-world stores, automatic international processing and currency exchange, and proprietary software tools for your business. While these additional offerings can be useful, they may also indicate that the vendor does not concentrate on the processing side, which may be all that you need.

◆ **Flexibility.** What cards or other forms of payment can the vendor handle? Depending on your customer base, you may need to process credit cards, debit cards, checks and money orders (mailed by customers who do not have or wish to use credit cards), and even cards denominated in foreign currency. Be careful when a vendor states that it accepts only certain cards or forms of payment now but expects to take others in the future. If you need the others, make sure that the vendor commits *in writing* to a date by which they will be accepted, or provides you with the ability to terminate and/or receive a refund if it fails to implement those methods in time.

◆ **Reports and assistance.** What kind of reporting and auditing will be available for you to track payments, review transaction histories, or track down errors? Does the vendor have client service representatives available throughout your business hours who can assist you in the event of suspected fraud or a problem with payment or processing?

Fraud and Cash Flow Concerns

WHAT KIND OF LEGAL RISKS CAN ARISE OUT OF AN INTERNET transaction-processing relationship? The key concerns are fraud and the possibility that you will not receive payment from the processor in time to pay your expenses. For retailers who don't keep inventory, requirements by card issuers that prohibit payment prior to shipment (or a short time before) can create a cash flow problem. The risks of customer fraud should be placed as much as possible on the processing company since it is in the business of evaluating claims for payment and presumably has adjusted its procedures, fees, and insurance coverage to account for a certain number of fraudulent card numbers and chargebacks. On the other hand, it is certainly reasonable, and expected, that the processing firm will require you to take certain steps on your own to detect and prevent fraud, and will hold you responsible if you fail to take those steps. Your agreement will probably obligate your company to

◆ compare given credit cards against the standard algorithms (to check for numbers which cannot be correct, because they do not follow card issuer patterns)

◆ keep a database of known fraudulent card numbers

◆ reasonably cooperate with any investigation by the processing company into alleged fraud, in order to be held harmless for undetected fraud.

The card issuer may also have specific guidelines and requirements, including verification of goods delivery in the event of a dispute, with which you may be required to comply as well. For its part, the processing firm should agree that, except in situations in which you have failed to meet your responsibilities, it will provide prompt payment of all charges to you, and that it will cooperate in any investigations you or your bank may conduct in connection with a purchase.

Proper Withholding of Sales Tax for Online Commerce

THE ONLINE COMMERCE SALES TAX QUESTION IS SIMILAR TO that faced by any catalog retailer: most states will require the collection of tax by any company with a business presence in the state in which the purchaser resides (or to which the goods are shipped). In other cases, although the consumer may be liable for so-called "use tax," the retailer is not responsible for collection or remittance of such tax. The unique question faced by online-only retailers is "Where am I doing business, when everything occurs online?" Imagine this scenario: an online bookseller has its corporate offices in New York, and its warehouse in Idaho, the only two facilities it operates. However, the server company from which the bookseller rents space has "server farms" in Pennsylvania, Montana, and Oregon, and the site is in fact mirrored in all three locations for reliability and speed of access. Further, the Internet service provider connecting the hosting company to the Internet is based in Cleveland, Ohio. For which of these locations, all directly involved in the operation of the Web site, is the retailer required to collect sales tax?

The best and most conservative answer is to follow the example set by the mail order firms, who also depend on everyone from printers to shipping companies to make their businesses run. Generally it is only the company's own facilities that are included in the calculation of taxable jurisdictions. In our example, the bookseller would probably have to collect tax for shipments to New York and Idaho, not any of the states in which the service providers operate. That does not mean that the other states will not try to require collection of tax; of course, all states wish to maximize their revenues, and many tax authorities have seen Internet commerce as an area ripe for passing tax rules which have not been successfully promulgated against mail-order companies. However, the trend to date among states such as California and the U.S. government has been against establishing Internet-specific taxes, choosing instead to apply the same standards to online businesses as for their real-world and mail-order retail cousins.

Calculating and collecting these taxes is usually done via mail-order business software. The software packages will normally come with periodic updates as local jurisdictions change tax rates and policies. As a reminder, be sure to carefully examine the agreements under which you license the taxation software to make sure that it will work with your shopping cart and processing packages. Also, you should obligate the service to provide you with frequent updates according to a fixed schedule, and the service should be liable for any tax penalties you accrue as a result of tax rate errors made by the service in its updates to you.

The preceding discussion has focused only on the sales

tax question within the United States. A multinational company with operations in regions that have alternate taxation schemes (such as the Value Added Tax charged by many countries) will need to investigate each jurisdiction's online commerce taxation policy. Your best approach is to work with an accounting firm with international experience; the research on sales tax (a common question) may be available to you at relatively low cost.

A Lot of Work in Store

THE CONCERNS ABOUT ONLINE RETAILING ARE NOT TREMENdously different from those of mall tenants or catalog publishers: turning people into shoppers, shoppers into buyers, and sales into profits. The differences stem in large part from the public, worldwide nature of the Internet, the lack of human interaction for much of the process (with an accompanying need for technical integration), and the ease of entry into the retailing space. Anyone with five megabytes of server space on America Online can theoretically begin selling online, although certainly without the kind of success earned by companies such as Amazon.com, which have invested millions of dollars in infrastructure, design, support, and advertising.

Despite the ease-of-entry benefits, though, no online retailing effort will succeed without real attention to detail and dedication to understanding and managing not only the day-to-day business of bringing in customers and selling them products, but the risks unique to Internet business. Retailing involves highly regulated areas such as product liability, consumer protection, and taxation. It is critical, therefore, that your effort be carefully planned and monitored, whether it's a stand-alone Web site or a "gift store" as part of a broader information or entertainment site. Otherwise, instead of selling your merchandise, you might be selling yourself short...or even being sold down the river.

A DAY ON THE LINKS

ALTHOUGH THE WORLD WIDE WEB TOOK A NUMBER OF YEARS
to approach its current worldwide status, it was a "web" from
the very start. The purpose of the Web when invented in
1991 by Tim Berners-Lee of the CERN physics lab was to
allow scientists to connect and link related documents,
hence the name *Web*. From the earliest adoption of HTML
and Web technology by others, this notion of linking has
become a major goal. Now users can click on text or images
and be transported seamlessly and instantly to another part
of the same site, or to some other site altogether. Linking is
the feature driving everything from online shopping malls to
search engines to online joint ventures to the navigation bars
found on most companies' Web sites.

It is technically simple to implement a link on a Web site:
the HTML code to link to the main page of the Web site for
this book, for example, is <A HREF= "http://www. click-
ingthrough.com">Clicking Through</A>. If you include this
text somewhere in the HTML of your Web page, it will display the words *Clicking Through*, which when clicked upon
will send the user away from your Web site to the Clicking
Through Web site, the same way as if the user typed the
Internet address into the browser. For your users to subsequently return to your site, they need either to click the
"Back" button on their browser, re-enter your address, or
click on a link to you on some other site.

A powerful way to attract your target audience is to
arrange links to your site on other sites to which your
desired users will go. On the other hand, you can get
burned if the link to your site is misleading, unflattering (as
in "Click Here for Lousy Customer Service"), or buried deep
within a list of similar sites in which your competitor is
prominently featured.

Why would you want to put links to others' sites on your
own? In the early, nonprofit days of the Web, having a list of
links was almost a requirement, as each user tried to teach
others about the "cool stuff" available online. Often a Web

site was little more than a personal biography and a book-mark list. In today's business world, though, sending a user to another site can not only be costly (since the user may not return), but even legally risky, as we'll see later in this section.

There are still good reasons for including a list or other forms of links to other Web sites. You may want to direct users to business partners or affiliates that operate separate sites, or may otherwise have a crosslinking arrangement with another company. You may operate a "portal" site, whose main purpose is to direct users to other Web sites (in exchange for promotional consideration or advertising revenue). There may be goods, services, or information that you do not wish to provide but that are available on other sites to which you provide links, a service you know will be useful for and appreciated by your target audience, who will return to your site for similar referrals. There are also "behind the scenes" HTML links possible, which your users may not even be aware of, enabling you to send your users to an online mall to process your retail orders or to bring in images such as comic strips from other Web sites, all the time appearing to provide the entire experience from your own Web server.

The business decision for linking your site with another is therefore not always an easy one, and it's complicated by some of the risks that have arisen both out of law and commercial reality. Linking can, if done improperly or even carelessly, result in loss of goodwill and customers, claims of intellectual property infringement, restraint of trade, or even criminal fraud. These kinds of cases tend to attract broad and unflattering headlines. What's worse, if you already have a Web site, it's almost a certainty that you have links on your site, often chosen by employees or designers who do not fully understand the legal and business risks involved.

The good news is that link liability is fairly easy to avoid entirely with a bit of care, and inappropriate linking is generally simple to discover as well. The clearest way to analyze the potential minefield is to look at the different types of linking and how they work, since each has its own characteristics. Once you understand the legal risks you face with each type of link, you can determine not only how best to establish links within your own site, but also under what circumstances (and with what conditions) you will permit or contract with other sites to link to yours. (See the checklists at the end of this chapter.)

The three usual types of linking are

1 Clickable links (text, graphics, or other objects)
2 Links embedded within HTML
3 Framing and client windows

Clickable Links

IN 1965, A RESEARCHER NAMED TED NELSON PUBLISHED AN article in which he described a method for linking related information from many different sources by means of not-yet-existing computer technology. Using these connections, which he called *hyperlinks,* a new form of multibranch "hypertext" would be created. Nelson continued to work on his hypertext "Xanadu," but his concept did not achieve commercial potential. That became possible with two developments: Tim Berners-Lee's creation of the Web; and students at the National Center for Supercomputer Applications at Urbana, Illinois writing Mosaic, the graphical Web browser program, which is the direct ancestor of both Netscape Navigator and Microsoft Internet Explorer. Today clicking on links is so ingrained in the computer user's consciousness that Microsoft included a Web browser interface for desktop components and files within the Windows 98 operating system.

The Pros and Cons of Requesting Permission to Link

IF YOU CHOOSE TO LINK TO ANOTHER SITE FROM YOUR OWN, you may be following the creative ideas of Nelson and Berners-Lee, but you may also be following the path to business and legal trouble.

The first question to ask is whether you need permission from the other site to include the link. In many cases, the answer is no: by choosing to place content on the World Wide Web, a site owner is essentially agreeing to the possibility that someone else will link to the content, whether directly or through one of the many search engines whose software automatically searches, reads, and indexes almost everything on the Web. If the content provider wants to put content online while preventing any kind of linking, there are a number of technical solutions, ranging from setting up a proprietary dial-up bulletin board service to redirecting any browsers coming from a link to another site.

In certain situations, though, obtaining permission is required or at least desirable, even when the linked-to content is freely available to users without technical impediment. One such scenario is when you place a link from your high-traffic site to a small, little-known Web resource. It is quite possible that the owner of the small site has intentionally chosen not to publicize its site, perhaps because it is meant for a limited audience, or because the site owner is paying its hosting company by the megabyte for all downloads beyond a fixed minimum. Your link and the resulting traffic could cost the smaller site users and money. Another potential problem arises when the site to which you link has a business arrangement, perhaps with one of your competitors, that grants exclusivity; even if the linked-to site did not initiate your link to it, the company's partner may object to a perceived breach of agreement.

An advantage of obtaining permission, particularly in writing, is that you can add provisions to the document, such as:

- a warranty from the other party that none of the content to which you are linking creates illegality or infringements
- indemnification in the event that you get sued for something done by the site to which you link
- the choice of law and forum for making the site and the governing rules for any disputes

Obtaining link permissions has some potential negative aspects. The first is that, in exchange for the granting of permission, the other party may demand contractual givebacks, compensation, or both from you. The second is perhaps more insidious: What happens if you try but can't get per-

Ticketmaster versus Microsoft

AMONG THE BEST EXAMPLES of a link-driven law-suit, illustrating how an aborted attempt at obtaining a linking agreement led to litigation, involved Ticketmaster, the national ticket broker, and Microsoft Corporation's Sidewalk Web site for the city of Seattle. According to press reports, Microsoft entered negotiations with Ticketmaster to provide direct ticketing services to Seattle-area sports events (such as Mariners games) to Sidewalk users in exchange for financial compensation from Microsoft. After the negotiations fell through, Microsoft went ahead and linked to the Ticketmaster site anyway, while Ticketmaster created an agreement with Citysearch, one of Microsoft's competitors in the localized Web site marketplace.

Ticketmaster subsequently sued Microsoft in May 1997 under a number of theories, ranging from wrongful appropriation and misuse of Ticketmaster's trademarks to unfair competition. According to Ticketmaster, the linking was made worse because the Sidewalk site provided links not only to Ticketmaster's home page, <http://www.ticketmaster.com>, but also to lower-level pages within Ticketmaster's site where users could purchase tickets. As a result, alleged Ticketmaster, users would fail to see the advertisements that Ticketmaster placed at the higher levels of its site, costing the company lost revenue.

Microsoft, in response, pointed out that it was not in fact accessing anything on Ticketmaster's site, but merely providing a link which the user could have just as easily typed in. Moreover, any time a user did select the Ticketmaster link within the Sidewalk site, that

mission? You may decide that you were overcautious in trying to obtain permission in the first place, and that you may place the link on your Web site even without formal approval. The difficulty here is that the other party has now user would be sent away from Sidewalk and to Ticketmaster, and might not return to Sidewalk. In addition, because Microsoft had no formal referral agreement with Ticketmaster, its choosing to make the link available could actually harm Microsoft financially rather than benefiting it, since Ticketmaster would receive 100 percent of any sales or repeat business arising out of the Microsoft link.

Microsoft also pointed out that, by virtue of how Web servers operate, Ticketmaster could easily detect when users were coming to its site via a link from Sidewalk, and redirect them to the top-level page of the Ticketmaster site. In fact, Ticketmaster eventually set up a redirect which intercepted all Sidewalk-linked users not to the main page, but to a page with a picture of a Dead End sign stating, "This is an unauthorized link and a Dead End for Sidewalk," without even a clickable link to the Ticketmaster home page. Some commentators pointed out that, from a strategic vantage, Ticketmaster's choice to block the Sidewalk users may actually have been more harmful than helpful, since it made it harder (rather than easier) for Microsoft-referred customers to complete ticket sales with Ticketmaster. Most also believed that the trademark-related claims made by Ticketmaster in its complaint were not at all strong, since Microsoft claimed no relationship with Ticketmaster, gained no profit from the referral, and did not highlight the Ticketmaster links prominently on the Sidewalk pages. The case was settled in February 1999 with Microsoft agreeing to remove the lower-level links.

been notified that you intended to get its permission, and will probably discover that you went ahead anyway without it, raising the possibility that the link could lead to your being sued. In the event that a lawsuit is filed against you, your attempt to contract for the link may well work against you in court as an admission that such permission was required (see the sidebar on the previous two pages).

What do you do if you want to place a link to another site on yours, but don't want to get a written agreement permitting the link (or think you will be unable to get the other party to sign one)? Essentially, the strategy is to assess the level of risk you face with the link, and take the best approach—between a written agreement and no efforts lie a number of different alternatives.

For example, you may choose to attempt a simple signed permission to link without the accompanying indemnification or warranty. This arrangement would be adequate if you are concerned about potential lawsuits from the site owner but not from third parties utilizing your link. The agreement might come in the form of an e-mail message (although depending on e-mail for contractual rights without authentication of the source is a bit risky). If you think the likelihood of lawsuit is minimal but want to ensure that any objections are expressed before linking (and that you won't overly inconvenience or damage the linked-to site), you can simply provide notice of your intention to establish the link to the other site owner, with a period of time for response after which the link will go live. Further along the spectrum is notice after the fact, with contact information in case the linked-to site owner wishes to correct or object to the link. Generally speaking, those companies who are most likely to be sued anyway (i.e., deep pocket or high-profile firms) should take a conservative approach to getting permissions for linkage.

Infringing—Prohibited Methods for Linking from (or to) Your Site

WHETHER OR NOT YOU OBTAIN OR EVEN NEED APPROVAL prior to establishing a link to another site, the question of the format of the link remains. This is in part a question of aesthetics and user interface design, but it additionally raises legal questions as well, primarily arising out of intellectual property law. From a copyright perspective, the same rules apply to linking as to any other use of copyrighted material such as text or graphics: absent a license or some fair use exception, the use of copyrighted works in the form of a link, whether to the author of the work or otherwise, may be an infringement. For example, it is generally not acceptable to use a scanned-in *Dilbert* comic strip as a link even to the official Dilbert site. Instead, often-linked sites like "The Dilbert Zone" may provide you with both acceptable (and licensed) artwork and specific guidelines for the use of the artwork as a link (see the sidebar on the following page).

The trademark issues are somewhat different, because trademark law does not prohibit all unauthorized uses of a mark in the same way that copyright law does for literary or artistic works. Instead, trademark infringement from links can occur either when a trademark is used incorrectly or negatively in connection with its owner or when one party's trademark is used to link to another's site.

In one example of (potential) trademark infringement arising out of a link, a major telecommunications company built a Web site intended as a community among its customers in 1995. On the site were areas related to home improvement, news, and entertainment, and at the top of one page there was a picture of the Starship Enterprise from *Star Trek* (owned by Paramount Pictures/Viacom) with a statement saying, "Do you like *Star Trek*? Click here." Unfortunately for the telecom company, the link was not to Paramount's official Star Trek site, but rather to a very well-designed but totally unauthorized site called "Federation Frontiers" designed and maintained by a then-Worcester Polytechnic Institute student named Ben Higgins. From a trademark perspective, while both Higgins and the telecom company might be deemed to have violated Viacom's trademarks by associating them with an unauthorized Web site (and copyrights by using images without permission), the vast likelihood was that, had Viacom chosen to sue, it would have brought its action not against the undergraduate but the wealthy, high-profile telecommunications company that (one would assume) had its own trademarks to protect and

The DilbertZone Link Guidelines

Go ahead, take one!

NOW YOUR SITE'S VISITORS can share in the fun of Dilbert. Link your site to <http://www.unitedmedia.com>, home of the Dilbert Zone, using one of the "Official Dilbert Link Icons" on this page. Use of these Icons is free to all but subject to the terms of the "Official Icon Link License Agreement" described below. Please be sure to read the agreement before downloading an Icon.

"DILBERT" OFFICIAL ICON LINK LICENSE AGREEMENT
    License. United Feature Syndicate grants to anyone using one of its DILBERT Icons (License) the nonexclusive right, until UFS gives notice to the contrary, to place the Icon in Licensee's web site, subject to the following conditions:
    (a) the Icon may be used only for the purpose of hyperlinking to UFS's sites at "http://umweb1.unitedmedia.com/comics/dilbert/" and/or "http://www.dilbert.com";
    (b) Licensee will not alter the appearance of the Icon in any manner; and
    (c) Licensee will make no use of any intellectual property of UFS, other than the Icon, without UFS's express written permission.

therefore should have known better. No action was ever publicly reported, the link was soon removed, and Mr. Higgins eventually shut his own site down, stating, "As of September 5, 1996, Federation Frontiers has been disbanded at the official request of Viacomm, Inc [sic] and the Paramount Pictures Corporation."

Of course, trademark law applies to the content of the site as well. It is just as impermissible to use your competitor's trademarks to identify your products in an online mall as it would be in a catalog, print ad, or real-world storefront. However, HTML makes some creative link-related infringements available which would not be possible in any other environment, such as the <meta> tag search-engine misdirection mentioned earlier in this chapter. Within HTML there are many tags allowing control over what the user sees on the screen; for example, the pair of tags <ul> </ul> around any text will cause the text to be underlined, and similarly <i> </i> will italicize text. In addition, there are a number of HTML tags that do not directly control screen display, but serve other command functions for Web browsers and servers, and <meta> is one such tag. The <meta> tag is used within an HTML document to provide useful information about the document rather than its content, such as the author of the page or language in which the page is written (helpful for text-to-speech translation software for visually-impaired users). Additionally, because the <meta> text is also part of the page read by each Web browser, it can provide direction to the automated Web indexing programs that generate the lists for such search engines as Altavista or Lycos, by describing some of the major categories the page will deal with. The World Wide Web Consortium (the official standards-setting body for HTML) has published the following information concerning HTML version 4.0:

META AND SEARCH ENGINES

A common use for META is to specify keywords that a search engine may use to improve the quality of search results. When several META elements provide language-dependent information about a document, search engines may filter on the lang attribute to display search results using the language preferences of the user. For example,

```
<— For speakers of US English —>
<META name= "keywords" lang= "en-us"
    content= "vacation, Greece, sunshine">
<— For speakers of British English —>
<META name= "keywords" lang= "en"
    content= "holiday, Greece, sunshine">
<— For speakers of French —>
<META name= "keywords" lang= "fr"
    content= "vacances, Gr&egrave;ce, soleil">
```

The effectiveness of search engines can also be increased by using the LINK element to specify links to translations of the document in other languages, links to versions of the document in other media (e.g., PDF), and, when the document is part of a collection, links to an appropriate starting point for browsing the collection.
<http://www.w3.org/TR/REC-html40/struct/global. html#edef-META>, accessed September 14, 1998.

One major and obvious choice for the <meta> text is the name of your company and its products. After all, if someone is using a search engine to try to find your site, it's likely that either company or product names will be part of the query. Some sites, though, have tried to increase their chances of coming up in a Web search by including not only their own product or company within the <meta> tag, but trademarks of a competing or otherwise unrelated firm as well. As a result, searches for the other companies would generate search-engine links to the infringing company's site, and the user might never realize that there was no relationship between the two. When this trademark inclusion (invisible to the users, but quite effective in the search engines) has been discovered by firms whose marks had been placed within the <meta> tag (or just as invisibly as black-on-black or white-on-white text within the page itself), a number have successfully brought lawsuits—including Playboy Enterprises (whose marks were used by an adult-content site) and even an Internet-savvy intellectual property law firm called Oppedahl and Larson (which found that its firm name was buried within a <meta> tag for a domain-name registration service). Once again, existing law was applied to the new technology of the Internet, and the same rules held.

Hot HTML: Stealing Others' Content for a Web Site

ALTHOUGH THE META TAG CAN LEAD INDIRECTLY TO AN infringing link, HTML permits more direct violation by automatically pulling graphics and other elements off one Web site onto another without permission, using the <img src => and other similar tags. Every Web page is made up of many different files, each with a distinct name and storage location. When a user clicks on a link, or types in a URL, the first thing received by the user is the complete HTML for the requested page, which may contain the text of the page but lack any graphics, images, or any content generated from databases. The browser software reads the HTML, and sends out requests in turn for each of the files named in the code. As a file is received, it is displayed to the user according to formatting instructions in the code. It's this multiple request process which makes "hits" a poor measurement of site audience, since each "hit" is a request for just one of the files on a page—a single user may be responsible for ten or more "hits" while reading just one multi-element Web page.

Usually, the files making up a Web site reside on a single server operated by (or for) the site owner, but they do not have to, and the user will not be aware if they don't. In some situations, a site may contract to pull in specific files from another location, including:

◆ ads served by networks such as DoubleClick
◆ stock quotes or specialized news feeds provided by informa-

tion services such as Reuters

◆ daily comic strips or columns provided by a syndicator

Even without permission or agreement, though, a Web site can load others' content into its page (or rather, can cause the user's browser software to combine the two sites' content into a single image) via HTML. In fact, any single file which can be retrieved by a browser program can be included within a Web page. A site choosing to do so, though, because its HTML code creates an audiovisual work using another company's proprietary content without authorization, risks actions for infringement of both copyright and trademark, even though the site may not have actually made or stored any copies of the materials on its own servers. The more proprietary the content included within the infringing site, the greater the potential penalties.

A site which hijacks content in this way can only be punished if it is caught. How are you to protect yourself against your Web site content being included by reference into someone else's Web page? How do you detect such a violation when it occurs? Does this mean that you shouldn't put any of your proprietary content onto your Web site?

A number of strategies can assist you in preventing and detecting content-jacking by another site owner:

◆ Try to place an identifying logo or other watermark within the visible portion of any graphic, demonstrating your ownership of the image.

◆ Give your sites individual files names which are not only descriptive of their content but which either include your company name or are otherwise easily searchable. (For example, have each file name include the same random string of characters, such as XR279G8.) Then, periodically use a search engine such as Altavista to find all sites whose HTML includes your chosen file identifier. Your site will certainly come up, so limit the search to exclude it in the results, but any site pulling your files in may also appear, allowing you to identify the offending parties.

◆ Make a habit of reviewing the access logs for your site, to see whether any one file on a particular page is downloaded significantly more than others on the page; that's an indication that a link to the file has been established by someone else.

♦ Use common sense. Some of your materials may be too sensitive to put on your Web site, since you cannot in fact prevent someone from copying and modifying your site's content offline. This is true whether or not the content is taken by another site via link or otherwise.

Frames on a Web Site

IMAGINE A PIRATE TELEVISION STATION WHOSE BROADCAST equipment was only four things: a TV set, a VCR, a camera, and a transmitter. What if the station's programming consisted of pointing the camera at the TV set and tuning the set to the most popular programs, with the pirate station's own commercials inserted in place of those of the channel being filmed? The pirate station could try to sell its advertising space on the basis of the top-rated programming it showed, and in fact might be able to demonstrate some audience figures to back up the claim. Nevertheless, this kind of retransmission of others' off-air signals would violate copyright, trademark, and a whole host of other laws. Even if the pirate station never actually recorded the other station's signals, rebroadcasting them live would not be tolerated.

A browser design decision by Netscape Communications Corp. has made an analogous process not only possible but popular within Web sites: the introduction of so-called *frames*. At their simplest, frames are windows within a browser window, established through special HTML commands, that can load content separately from the surrounding window. In other words, within a frame on a Web page there can be content from elsewhere within that site, or even entirely from another site, and links contained within the frame will cause new content to be loaded upon clicking. In many instances, frames are used quite creatively and usefully by Web sites. Some put navigation buttons along the side of the window, which link to different site sections within a large adjacent frame, or allow users to refer quickly to relevant information placed elsewhere without leaving the main site.

What happens, though, when a site builds the Web analog of the pirate television station described above, perhaps by designing a Web page which is almost entirely a frame except for a small advertising banner along the bottom? Because of the browser features, although the content may be that of the "framed" site, the address bar at the top of the screen identifies the "framing" (pirate) site; in addition, selecting the "Add Bookmark" or "Add Favorite Place" command from the pull-down menus will store a link not to the framed site but to the framing site. The pirate site may also be able to report user views on its advertising that are generated not by its own content, but from the framed site, which receives no compensation.

Unlike tracking file hijackers, discussed above, detecting unauthorized framing is much more difficult. Searching for a URL linking to your site is not always exact.

If you can find a site framing yours directly, and want to take action to stop it or at least to be compensated, what choices do you have? In one highly publicized case, news providers took both technical and legal approaches to prevent the framing of their sites by a Web site called Total-News. The TotalNews site had three frames: a menu bar of logos from approximately ten news Web sites (such as CNN and ABC News) along the left side, a banner ad from a Total-News advertiser at the bottom, and a main window in which the news sites would appear when their logos were clicked. The framed sites would appear in full, directly from their host servers, although the reduced size of the frame meant that a user often had to slide a scroll bar to see the entire page. A casual observer might have concluded, based upon the limited number of sites featured, that TotalNews had a business relationship with those site owners; however, a disclaimer three levels down within the TotalNews site indicated that no such relationship existed.

When the site was discovered, the debate among online businesses focused on whether the benefit gained, since the frames included all advertising for the linked-to sites, outweighed whatever revenue TotalNews gained from its advertisers. Some worried that, were TotalNews to be prohibited from operating with its framed interface, other sites might find even simple linking forbidden.

The news sites themselves, though, chose two routes to object to TotalNews's activities. In February 1997 many joined together to bring a lawsuit against TotalNews, claiming misappropriation of copyright and trademarks. This suit was ultimately settled when TotalNews agreed to stop framing the plaintiffs' sites (although it continued to frame other, nonlitigating sites). At the same time, CNN addressed the technical innovation of the TotalNews frame with one of its own: it embedded code within its site's HTML which, when loaded into a frame, would cause the framed site to fill the entire browser window, effectively breaking the frame. TotalNews remains in operation, combining framing and nonframing, while continuing to sell advertising banners.

One more important point about frames—although a site can choose to which sites it directly links within a frame, it is impossible to prevent users from clicking on links within the linked-to page to go to other sites or even search engines, which open up the entire Web. However, this secondary framing is not likely to result in legal liability. After all, if you don't provide a direct link, it would be difficult to argue that you intended users to go to a specific site. On the other hand, though, it is entirely plausible that your site's frame, with your company name on it, could end up framing content that was inappropriate, illegal, or simply not material for your company's purposes. What happens if a child goes from a frame within your site to pornographic material, and a parent walks in to see your company's logo surrounding the photos? Imagine, too, if a magazine or your competitor published a picture of a browser window with your site framing something inappropriate or embarrassing. Unfortunately, if you choose to implement frames within your Web site, the *only* way to prevent such occurrences is to ensure that there are *no* links to inappropriate sites or pages from any of the pages to which you link, or any of the pages to which those pages themselves link, and to keep checking that the linked-to pages haven't changed to include outside links.

Building Proper Links

LINKING, FRAMING, AND HTML PULLS CAN BE PART OF ANY Web site with a minimum of legal and business risk if done properly. As a site owner, you need to be concerned with two different aspects: how to properly link to other sites, and with what to be concerned when other sites link to you. Here is a pair of checklists:

ESTABLISHING LINKS TO OTHER SITES

◆ Why do you want to establish the link? Will it cost you more in lost repeat users than it will net in increased initial visits and goodwill?

◆ Do you need permission to establish the link? It is more necessary to obtain permission if

—your company is a well-known, deep-pocket firm which is frequently the target of nuisance suits

—you expect heavy traffic on your Web site, enough to overwhelm smaller sites to which you might link

—you have previously negotiated some business relationship with the other site (or its owner) that was unconsummated

—the other site is doing business, or considering doing business, with one of your competitors

— your site design lends the impression that you have business relationships with the linked-to sites (e.g., only a few, well-highlighted links)

—the linked-to page has controversial, age-sensitive, or everchanging content (in which case you might want to add disclaimers and warranties to your permission agreement)

◆ Do you need actual signed written permission? If the risk of damages and/or lawsuits from the link is not serious, consider written notification of the link as an alternative.

◆ Is the link you made in the proper form and format? Some issues we've discussed include:

—unauthorized use of trademarks and copyrighted work

—misleading or incorrect information contained within a link

Clicking Through: Some Contractual Language for Cross-Linking

◆ **Approval of Location of Link.** Prior to a party placing the other party's Link into the designated page on the placing party's Web Site, or relocating an existing Link to a new location on the same page or another page, the placing party shall provide the other party with written and disk-based copies of the proposed page (or pages) which include(s) the Link. The location or relocation shall be deemed approved unless the other party provides written notice of its disapproval to the placing party within five (5) business days after receipt of such proposed page. If the other party shall not approve a page, the parties agree to work together in good faith to revise the proposed page or relocate the Link to an agreed-upon page. In the event that the parties cannot agree on such revision or relocation within thirty (30) days, this Agreement shall be terminated in accordance with the termination provisions set forth below. Notwithstanding the foregoing, a party shall not be obligated to receive the other party's approval for changes to the Web Page that do not materially alter the location or context of the Link.

91

◆ **Characteristics of Links.** Each Link to be provided hereunder shall be provided in electronic form and shall consist of a banner and a textual reference, together with a current HTML-formatted address pointing to the providing party's Web Site. A Link may not incorporate any illegal or offensive material, and a party may reject any Link that (in its reasonable judgment) contains such material. Each party shall, within five (5) days of the execution of this Agreement, provide the other party with any additional technical specifications for the Link to enable the Link to be placed on such party's Web Site.

—behind-the-scenes HTML links which fail to show the content's origin

—frames which mislead users into assuming a business relationship, or which illegally trade on another's trademarks or content for commercial gain

◆ Have you checked any links already on your site for the above problems?

◆ Do you have procedures in your site maintenance plan to regularly check your links for changes to the pages or their addresses, to avoid dead or incorrect links?

DEALING WITH SITES THAT LINK TO YOURS

◆ Are you frequently checking for unknown or incorrect links to your sites using search engines and other methods (such as employee incentives for discoveries)?

◆ Are you reviewing your access log to detect content-jacking through another site's HTML code, which pulls one of your files without the surrounding page from your server?

◆ Do you insist on obtaining permission in all cases prior to the establishment of links? (If so, remember that you will be expected to grant the same rights to all sites to which you yourself link.)

◆ Have you requested (or required) approval rights over the content in which a link to your site will be placed and to the form and format of the link itself?

◆ Under what circumstances would you want to terminate a link to your site? Do you have the power to obligate the linking site to remove the reference? If not, what will you do if they refuse to pull the link down?

CHAPTER 2

Internet Opportunities=Company @ Risk

ADVERTISING
FOR TROUBLE

HE PREVIOUS CHAPTER DISCUSSED LINKING
one site to another using different types of HTML
formatting codes. One of the major reasons for
linking your site to another relates to another kind
of link—the traditional one between advertisers and
the media. Newspapers, buildings, and television
have long sold space or time to businesses, and the
Web offers additional ways to reach consumers.

The flexibility of Internet formatting and technology applies equally to Web advertising. There are
almost as many types of Web-based advertising
methods as there are Web sites. However, the vast
majority of Web ads fall into several categories.

◆ **Banner ad.** Perhaps the most familiar form of Web
advertising. The banner ad is a stand-alone image or

animation placed on a Web page, often at the top or bottom, or within a navigation bar alongside the page. The ad is usually a clickable link to the advertiser's Web page, or to a dedicated page within the site on which the ad is placed, and may also include actual functionality (real-time information display, pull-down lists, or even "Buy Me" options for products). A few groups, most notably the Internet Advertising Bureau (in conjunction with the advertising trade association known as Coalition for Advertising Supported Information and Entertainment, or CASIE) have sought to standardize the available sizes for banner ads to simplify the design process and to allow price comparisons across different Web sites. The IAB/CASIE standards, measured in pixels, can be found at <http://www.iab.net/iab_banner_standards/bannersizes.html>. Banner ads actually predate the Web: proprietary online services such as

Prodigy had banner-like ads well before Tim Berners-Lee launched his novel communications tool.

◆ **Advertorial.** The term *advertorial* refers to content on a Web site (or in any other medium) provided by an advertiser as part of (or in exchange for) its compensation to the site owner, generally along with attribution to the advertiser on the site. For example, a sneaker manufacturer could offer a monthly column on running to an online women's magazine. For the advertiser, advertorials provide brand building with lower costs than with straight advertising, and may also enable the advertiser to subtly push its products within the column. The site owner may receive less cash from advertorials, but in exchange, it is also spared some of the labor and financial burden of refreshing and supplementing the site's content.

◆ **Sponsored areas or events.** Many sites, rather than deferring their costs through advertising placement, will follow the public television model of obtaining sponsors for blocks of content, again accompanied by credit. The sponsorship may cover an area on the Web site, real-world and/or online events put on by the site owner, or both.

◆ **Interstitial advertising.** These Web site ads are the online analogue to television commercials, and are placed between Web pages rather than on them. In other words, when a user clicks on a link or types in a URL, the user is first shown an ad for a specified amount of time, after which the ad goes away and the desired page loads. Interstitials are often found on sites which have a specific path for users to follow, such as Berkeley Systems' *You Don't Know Jack* online quiz show found at <http://www.bezerk.com>. Interstitials appeal to advertisers, because they provide sole presence on the screen. They also appeal to site designers, particularly of the more esoteric sites, because there's no need to make room in the site interface for a banner. Users, though, are not always comfortable with the perception that the site takes over their browser to "show a commercial."

The advertising-driven revenue model was the earliest and is still probably the most prevalent choice for those Web site owners wishing to generate cash directly from their sites. It certainly is easier to implement than an online store, and doesn't require you to convince users to pay a subscription or download fee (difficult even for established publishers, and almost impossible for newly launched efforts). Actually, the only sites that have garnered significant subscribers are niche-market services, which charge lower fees for Web access to their content than for the print or proprietary online versions, and sex-related sites.

Many Web site owners have been less than successful in meeting their revenue targets from online advertising sales. Much of the failure is because the business case for buying online rather than traditional ads has not been proven to many advertisers' satisfaction, even though the demographic data for Web users are far more detailed than that for television or even print consumers. In some cases, though, the weakness of the online advertising revenue stream arises out of the unique challenges and legal risks associated with the process. What is it about online advertising that poses such unique risks? The answers range from the technological requirements to the legal aspects of advertising which were not created with the Web in mind. In this section we will focus on the following significant sources of legal risk from creating or accepting online ads:

- ◆ Control over ad content and placement
- ◆ Clickthrough arrangements
- ◆ International consumer protection laws and regulations
- ◆ The unintended effects on existing contracts of being an instant global marketer.

The Challenges of Remotely Supplied Banner Ads and Changing Page Content

IMAGINE SUBSCRIBING TO A MAGAZINE WITH ADVERTISEMENTS that arrived separately in the mail, with instructions on where to paste them in. Beyond the inconvenience to the consumer, no magazine would accept such an arrangement, even were it practical, if only because magazines and other media outlets need to know that the advertisements they run follow certain standards of acceptability. For example, the *New York Times* would probably not accept an ad for whoopee cushions (unless they were embossed with the *Times'* crossword puzzle, of course). It wouldn't fit with the image of the publication, and would likely offend its more stodgy readers. Similarly, a right-wing radio program might decline to run Amnesty International appeals, and a Sunday morning prayer show would likely refuse 900-number adult chat line ads. The advertisers in these instances would probably never pursue these opportunities anyway, since the recipients of the ads would not be their intended customers.

The same hypothetical after-mailing combining of ads and text, which is unimaginable for a magazine, happens every day on Web sites. Consider this: because each Web page is made up of many different files, which can come from many different locations, there is nothing stopping an advertiser from providing ads "on the fly" each time a user clicks to receive the page on which the ad has been placed. Why would an advertiser do this? Because serving the ads directly allows an advertiser to ensure the prices in the ad are absolutely current, and even to perform real-time market research: Does placing the graphic on the left side of the banner produce more clicks than if it were on the right? Which of the three different versions of a sales pitch appeals most to women between the ages of 18 and 35? Ad serving also allows an advertiser to quickly change from advertising an out-of-stock item to one that is over-inventoried. It's power which has never before existed in the hands of advertisers, but that is almost effortless on the Web.

For a site owner, having remotely served ads reduces the bandwidth load on the site owner's own server, particularly when a graphic-rich ad takes longer to download than the rest of the site's text. It also lowers the site owner's exposure for technical, factual, or intellectual property infringement problems in the ads, since it may never actually view or store them, but rather make a place on a page where the ads will be displayed when the advertiser transmits them.

At the same time, a site owner can be burned by having ads remotely served by the advertiser, for the same reasons as in our magazine hypothetical—no ability to monitor compliance with standards. If your Web site has certain requirements and prohibitions and an advertiser sends you a banner ad that violates those standards, you can require changes prior to putting the ad online. If the advertiser is serving the ad in real-time from its own server, though, the first time you know about a standards violation may be when you get the first call (or hundred calls) from your unhappy consumer—or from a prosecutor. By that point, the genie is out of the bottle, and all that you can do is damage control. Even placing explicit standards in your advertising agreement will not prevent an advertiser from serving inappropriate ads; it will only provide you with some additional remedies if problems arise.

The control problem happens for the site owners only when ads are remotely served. You should realize, though, that online advertisers face this situation with every placement of every ad, whether or not done in real time, because sites themselves can change weekly, daily, or even minute by minute. On some sites, in fact, it's not even the site owner who controls what the user will see, but the user himself (through methods such as expressed preferences, tracked behavior, and chat room conversation). The advertiser has no certainty as to the context in which its advertisement will be seen. If you are the online advertiser, you must ensure through explicit contractual language that whatever placement requirements you expect (top half of page, no ads surrounding yours, no inappropriate content to be served with your ad) is written into the insertion order.

Clickthrough Ad Payment Deals

THERE'S ANOTHER SITUATION IN WHICH LACK OF CONTROL over ad content can have major financial impact: when a Web site and an advertiser agree on a clickthrough requirement for payment, the inspiration for the title of this book. In clickthrough, the ad is served a specific number of times or for a predetermined period without charge to the advertiser. However, each time a user clicks on the ad (or, in some cases, follows through with a purchase on the advertiser's site or otherwise interacts with the advertiser), the site on which the ad is placed gets paid. These types of deals, which are clearly more beneficial to the advertiser than the site, are generally found among the larger and more powerful advertisers who have the leverage to push through such deals. Procter & Gamble, one of the single largest advertisers in the world, was among the first to announce a clickthrough arrangement on the Yahoo! Web site in April 1996, an event which caused a great deal of commotion among site owners and advertisers alike (see <http://www2.nando.net/news-room/ntn/info/042896/info5_380.html> for details). Even if a site owner is willing to agree to the inherent risk of a clickthrough, lack of control over ad content can cause further complications. For example, imagine that you make a deal with an athletic shoe company to put a banner ad on your site, and agree, because of the prestige of the shoe company and other business you wish to do with it, to charge only for clickthroughs on the banner. What if, after the contract is signed, the advertiser presents you with a banner ad which, while lauding the advertiser's brand, has absolutely no pull or even an indication that the advertiser wants users to click the banner for more information? You're left with a choice of breaching the contract by refusing to run the ad, or running it at an almost-guaranteed loss. In either case, your relationship with your sponsor is soured, and you've likely lost money as well.

Instead of risking conflict by not addressing these concerns, plan ahead with a specialized clickthrough agreement which meets them head on. A good agreement will include:

◆ A careful definition of exactly which event or events (view of ad, click on banner, making initial purchase, making subsequent purchases) will trigger compensation

◆ A reliable mechanism for tracking and recording clicks

◆ A specific time frame for payments (potentially including audit rights to detect underpayments)

◆ Specifications for the ads and content, both in size and in appropriate subject matter

◆ Reasonable power for the site to review the content and specific reasons why it may reject or modify the banner (for example, if the banner does not invite users to click on it).

Although these types of provisions won't eliminate the possibility that you will get into a clickthrough-related conflict, even the process of negotiating a clickthrough agreement can help you decide whether you wish to go through with the deal and, if so, where the problems may arise.

Liability without Boundaries: International Advertising

MANY PEOPLE MAY JOKE THAT RUNNING TOO MANY COMMERcials during their favorite TV show is a crime; the fact is, however, that there are many laws, regulations, and self-regulatory policies governing the content, presentation, and target for advertising. In the United States, most advertising is governed by the Federal Trade Commission, state legislation, attorneys general, and the courts. Advertiser-supported self-control efforts include such groups as the National Advertising Division of the Council of Better Business Bureaus (usually referred to by its initials, the NAD, and whose procedures can be found online at <http://www.bbb.org/advertising/nadproc.html>). Most advertisers and media outlets are aware of these bodies and their standards, and probably have internal guidelines designed to insure or maximize the chances of compliance with the relevant standards bodies.

Unfortunately for those companies that have until now been U.S. only, and have crafted their advertising accordingly, the Internet once again poses new and perhaps serious challenges. It opens the possibility that authorities all over the world will be reviewing, and perhaps prosecuting based upon, any advertising placed within a Web site. Remember that prohibitions on false or misleading advertising and other advertising-related laws, like many other consumer protection efforts, are usually concentrated locally, since the crime is deemed to occur where the victims are, rather than only where the perpetrator is located. As a result, prosecutors and legislators from Munich to Minsk could decide that your advertisement is illegal under their local laws, and seek to penalize you for it.

What kind of advertising can run afoul of foreign law?

Here are a few general examples:

◆ Comparative advertising of your products versus other named products is illegal in a number of countries, and sharply limited in others.

◆ For heavily regulated products and services from insurance to pharmaceuticals, you can anticipate disclosure requirements, limitations on claims, prohibitions on the sale of certain products, and similar issues; these may be different for each jurisdiction.

◆ Laws, especially those related to intellectual property, and local artists guild regulations can affect which photos, videos, and sounds are permissible in advertising, and whether compensation is due the artist, publisher, and/or talent for the use.

Obviously, if you put either a banner ad or a reproduction of a print or broadcast advertisement on your Web site, you can expect that advertising regulation will come into play, and need to plan accordingly. Remember, though, that advertising is in the eye of the beholder. In other words, even if you have nothing you'd recognize as an ad on your site, the mere fact that you have created the site for your company might turn it into a very large ad in the opinion of a local law enforcement or artists guild official. Either way, the effort to research and navigate foreign jurisdictions' advertising laws can be costly and time-consuming.

Is the potential for unintentionally violating foreign law likely for you? If your business is entirely local, and you will never solicit or accept either suppliers or customers or establish offices outside the United States, the power of foreign regulators is probably limited. Of course, criminal activity could subject you to an extradition effort, but few advertisements rise to that level. On the other hand, if you are international, or foresee the possibility of establishing strong international ties in the future, you must pay attention to issues such as foreign advertising law. Your Web site could cause legal complications for your company, one of your affiliates, or customers. The last thing you want for your premiere event in a new foreign office is pending criminal prosecution.

What can you do to prevent international advertising-related problems? To some extent, the best approach is a conservative one, both in the elements you include in your Web site and the claims that you make within it. Just as a domestic advertisement in a general-interest publication would probably not be made too risqué, for fear of offending potential customers, so too advertising copy on a Web site should be scrutinized for potential controversy. Ultimately, you may choose to leave in a controversial element because you believe your target audience will respond to it positively, but at least make an informed decision, preferably with the assistance of advisers knowledgeable in international advertising regulations.

Once you have identified your target audience, explicitly state it in your site's disclaimer language and other places likely to be read by users (and regulators). For example, many commercial sites created by U.S. companies state, "Information contained in this site concerning any products and services is meant for U.S. residents only." To help ensure that the site will be interpreted as you expect it to be, it is wise to add language that "This site and its contents and any transactions taking place herein shall be governed by the substantive laws of the State of _____, United States of America, excluding principles of conflicts of laws, and the exclusive forum for any disputes arising out of this site shall be the state and federal courts located in the City of _____, State of _____." You may be familiar with provisions like these in your business contracts. In fact the goal is always to make your disclaimers as enforceable as a contract, even if it's never actually "signed" by the user. Unfortunately, there's no guarantee that a court or regulator would accept these provisions as binding, but having them readily visible on your site is a step in the direction of addressing foreign regulations.

What if you don't want your site to be considered advertising, as, for example, if you are building an industry resource or news site? Beyond the legal issues, there are many reasons to avoid classification as an advertisement, such as the increased cost for talent releases or copyright licenses when materials are used for commercial purposes.

Commercializing News, or Newsworthy Ad? Drawing a Fuzzy Line

THE DISTINCTION BETWEEN commercial and editorial content is never a clear one. For example, few would doubt that the *New York Times* or CNN are intended as news outlets, but they are also for-profit efforts that spend millions of dollars each year building their brand, including house ads mixed in with their own news stories. Similarly, advertisements at times can be incredibly factual and informative, from the specifications for a new car to the list of side effects printed in a drug ad.

How can you tell whether something will be considered news or hype? The answer depends on the particular use of material and how it relates to the whole publication or broadcast. For example, *Time* magazine would not need to get clearance from actor Charlton Heston in order to put his picture on the cover to illustrate a story about his presidency of the National Rifle Association. On the other hand, if Heston were not mentioned in the magazine at all but were still on the cover, or if he were depicted reading *Time* in a print ad attached to a subscription card, his permission and payment to him would likely be required. Courts also examine elements such as how much of a copyrighted work is taken (or how prominently a famous person is featured) and the usual function of the media property that used the proprietary material without prior consent. The law does provide some guidance, but no clear-cut guidelines.

When attempting to avoid your site's being characterized as advertising, the best approach is to spell out your intentions throughout the site as clearly as possible, and hope that regulators will agree. While a site's disclaimer can state that "this site is for informational purposes only," this will generally not be enough to convince an attorney general, prosecutor, or guild representative that you're a reporter rather than an advertiser. Instead, examine the impression that the site as a whole provides to an outside observer:

◆ Are many manufacturers' products/services described or just yours (or your sponsors')? How many of your articles are advertorials? Are they clearly labeled as such, and distinguished from the other content?

◆ Are the authors and editors of your site's content applying newspaper-like standards of source integrity, fact-checking, and proper attribution to their works?

◆ Does your site display an overall purpose other than (or in addition to) saying, "buy this"?

In this type of inquiry, it is often helpful to enlist outsiders to look through the site and describe their overall impressions. Attorneys who have tried intellectual property cases related to advertising can be good choices, as can newspaper editors or journalists or television producers accustomed to making these distinctions in their own work. Whatever the conclusion, though, always keep in mind that someone such as a foreign regulator may deem your site advertising and therefore subject to applicable consumer protection and intellectual property laws. You should have at least the bare bones of a contingency plan in the event this happens.

A World of Trouble—Global Web Ads

EVEN IF YOUR SITE OR YOUR ADVERTISEMENTS ON ANOTHER Web site run into no regulatory problems, the global reach of Internet advertising can cause other legal and business headaches for the unwary company. Among the most overlooked areas for potential risk is in marketing and sales agreements and licenses, which quite often contain clear geographic limitations. If you have that type of agreement or some other preexisting relationship with geographic limitations on your sales, you must take extra care when crafting and publishing a Web site.

Here are a few examples of the types of contracts and arrangements to which your company might be a party, and how a Web site can cause you to breach them:

◆ **Franchise and sales representative agreements.** Franchisers have taken action against franchisees or sales representatives who have built their own Web sites, alleging not only that the sites violated corporate guidelines for product descriptions or pricing, but also that the franchisee or rep has begun marketing beyond its set location, potentially endangering the livelihood of other franchisees around the world.

◆ **Trademark or copyright use licenses.** Many companies have licensed their brand or product names from or to other firms, sometimes in foreign countries. These agreements generally require noncompeting use, usually with geographic limitations. Imagine that a customer in the licensor's country types the product name into a search engine, and ends up on the licensee's site—the licensor will not be happy to lose the local sale. Copyright, guild, and author agreements price worldwide usage substantially differently, and higher, than domestic reproduction does. If the agreement does not specifically permit Web usage, placing a domestic-only work on a Web server can very well be deemed an immediate breach of the license.

◆ **Pricing relationships with distributors or manufacturers.** Manufacturers selling products internationally know that countries have very different pricing requirements. Standard of living, currency valuations, and tariffs all contribute to charging varying amounts for the same goods in different countries. It is in the manufacturers' best interests for retailers to keep such pricing differences hidden from customers to avoid confusion or bad feelings. Pricing terms often require this geographic limitation. As more and more retail-related Web sites begin including price lists, though, these differences can cause grief to both manufacturers and local salespeople. Imagine a U.S. customer trying to negotiate a lower price because the same product is on sale for less in an emerging country. However, the typical per capita income is one-tenth that in the United States, and the manufacturer sells at a loss there in order to establish a market presence. Alternatively, consider the resentment that a consumer in a tariff-heavy country may feel to see U.S. pricing that is 50 percent lower.

If you are faced with this potential situation when building your Web site, you should contact the relevant contracting party to discuss what you can do to minimize problems. The party may ask you to keep your Web site from users outside your geographic limits. Unfortunately, technical limitations may keep you from reliably blocking access to your site from outside your territory or region, because it is impossible for Web server software to identify a user's country of origin. Even though users' computers are identified by IP addresses when they access the Internet, the address can be traced not to the user but only to the Internet service provider or company providing connectivity. Once an IP address is identified to a particular person by some other means (for example, if the user types in an address in response to an online sales solicitation), it can then be associated with that person in a database, and the server will know from whom and where a communication comes. Most ISPs, though, issue IP addresses "dynamically," with a fixed collection of IP addresses doled out to users on a first-come, first-served basis and returned to the "bank" for re-use when that particular user logs off. Because the largest ISPs, such as America Online or CompuServe, may have customers all over the world, the same IP address may correspond on Monday to a user in Albuquerque, and on Tuesday to someone else in Milan. Even if a user is assigned a fixed IP address, the user may be accessing the Internet on a laptop computer, carried across borders into restricted areas.

Some sites have adopted one or more techniques to combat this problem, including:

◆ A main home page with links to areas or other sites targeted at each country or region. Possibly all other pathways into the site will be redirected to that entry page in order to force every user to "pass the guardpost," requiring users to click to choose the region in which they are located. Nothing can prevent a user from entering false information to gain access to other areas of the site.

◆ A database search on the IP address to at least pinpoint the geographic location of the ISP, if not the user. This is useful for reducing the possible violations, since most users are physically in the same region as their ISP. For subscribers to the national and international ISPs and employees of multi-national companies gaining access from work, however, this technique can be close to useless.

◆ Third-party verification (e.g., credit card numbers, verification of multiple information types such as name, address, and telephone number) akin to that used by the sex-related sites, but also prone to potential for fraud.

Online Advertising Checklists

FOR THE ADVERTISER

◆ What is your goal in placing the ad?
  —Overall brand building?
  —Encouraging users to enter your own Web site?
  —Direct retail sales?
◆ What kind of ad will best achieve that goal?
  —Banner
  —Interstitial
  —Advertorial
  —Sponsorship
  —Other
◆ How is the site on which your ad is placed measuring success/number of users?
  —CPM (Cost per thousand users, equivalent to traditional advertising?)
  —Page views?
  —Unique users?
  —Clickthroughs?
  —Retail sale referred through the ad?
◆ Has the site provided you with specifications (technical requirements, file size, image size) prior to designing the ad?
◆ Does the site have sufficient auditing tools/third party confirmation to back up its volume claims? Do you have access to those tools? Do you understand how they record information and what assumptions they make about user behavior?
◆ Are you going to try to negotiate a clickthrough arrangement with the site? If so, what control can the site exercise over

your content?

- If your ad will be served by the site, can you get any guarantees regarding reliability of the site's servers?
- If your ad is in rotation with others, how often will it be seen? Will it be matched with your competitors, and is that a problem for you?
- Can you put in place any requirements for the content in which your ad will be featured? Can the site owner even control the content? Can you get review and rejection rights?
- If you are serving your ads locally, have you arranged for sufficient backup and bandwidth to guarantee that your ad will always be sent when requested by the site?
- What are the international issues with which you must be concerned?
- Does your company have or plan any operations or affiliations overseas?
- Is there anything in your ad which might cause foreign regulators to take action?

FOR SITE OWNERS ACCEPTING ADVERTISING

- What kind of ads will your users respond to favorably? Which will cause bad feelings?
- How will the advertiser treat those users referred from your site (could they generate bad will against you)?
- Are the editorial areas of your site sufficiently differentiated from the advertisements such that users and regulators will know the difference?
- What standards should advertisers follow when creating ads for your site? What are your rights in the event you strike a clickthrough deal? What enforcement rights do you have (by contract or law) against advertisers who do not follow your guidelines?
- Are your ad revenue projections realistic? If you don't meet them do you have a contingency plan for utilizing the unsold ad inventory or otherwise generating income?
- Do your site's disclaimers contain the appropriate warnings, target audience, and jurisdictional language?

WHEN IN DOUBT, DON'T

ULTIMATELY, THE LACK OF GEOGRAPHIC LIMITS THAT MAKES
the Web such an enticing place to do business can cause real
problems for advertisers and marketers. Businesses must be
prepared to manage the relationship appropriately to market
to the world in this way. When the risk is particularly serious, and the techniques to prevent it uncertain enough to
provide the comfort level your situation requires, you may
choose to limit your use of the Web for advertising purposes.
Remember, though, that even without placing or accepting a
single ad, the Web and the rest of the Internet still provide
countless opportunities for both making and saving money
for your business.

CREATING WIN-WIN SWEEPSTAKES

WHAT NEED DO OWNERS OF INTERNET WEB SITES SHARE?
In a word, traffic. Getting initial and, more importantly,
repeat visits is crucial to a site's success.

Web sites use a number of techniques for bringing in
"eyeballs," including:

◆ Compensation to users, from frequent flier miles (Click-
Rewards, at <http://www.clickrewards.com>) to buying
points (the MyPoints site, <http://www.mypoints.com>) to
actual cash (Cybergold's program, found at <http://www.
cybergold.com>)

◆ Traditional advertising, for example, television commercials for search sites such as Yahoo!, Lycos, and Hotbot, or
the Priceline.com campaign starring actor William Shatner

◆ E-mail announcements with newsletters or regular bulletins of sales (like the weekly Overstocks bargains from
Lands' End <http://www.landsend.com>) or unsolicited
and often-criticized "spam" e-mail for sex-related or other
sites

◆ Banner ads and the other site-to-site advertising methods.

Besides these common tools for gathering a Web site audience, one more set of techniques, notable both for their popularity and unique legal requirements, are sweepstakes, contests, or other prize promotions.

Prize promotions are popular for a few reasons. First and foremost, they work. People are always intrigued by the possibility of winning a prize for little or no effort, and the expectation among many Web users that everything online is free fits in well with this. Also, promotions have the benefit that (as they say on TV commercials pitching sweepstakes at children) "many will enter, but few will win." Unlike activities for online retail discount or other traffic-generation, the vast majority of users who enter a Web sweepstakes will not receive any compensation, nor will they expect any.

Beyond the cost of the prizes (which may even be donated by cosponsors), Web-based promotions are among the lowest-cost and easiest-to-manage traffic enhancers around. They require little or no adjustments to your day-to-day business, have predictable start and end dates, and can often be outsourced to specialized contest firms such as Marden-Kane (<http://www.mardenkane.com>), which will handle everything from obtaining the prizes to advertising the promotion to reviewing the legality of the rules (more about that later). Moreover, there are a number of specialized magazines and Web sites (such as Sweepstakes Online, <http://www.sweepstakesonline.com>) devoted to tracking promotions for prospective entrants that can do a better job of publicizing your sweepstakes than you could ever do.

If there is a downside to running a promotion like a sweepstakes, particularly online, it is that the ease and low cost do not free you from often-onerous regulation. The laws regarding giveaways and contests fall under the consumer protection umbrella, and are very localized. In the United States, these rules are the purview of individual states, most of which have similar, but not identical, laws, and backed up by the interstate commerce regulations of the Federal Trade Commission. Unfortunately, a few states have made a name for themselves for making it difficult or even illegal to run certain common types of promotions. As with everything else about the Internet, though, an online promotion from a U.S. company is immediately available not only within the United States but all over the world, and internationally there is little or no uniformity regarding promotions laws and enforcement. Some countries place power locally, others in national bodies. Each region will also have its own rules about the types and value of prizes to be awarded, the tasks required for a resident of that region to win the prize, and any bonding or other financial obligations imposed upon the company running the promotion.

Thankfully, Internet businesses find it much easier to make an Internet sweepstakes legal than to conform to other kinds of consumer-protection regulatory regimes with online advertising. Sweepstakes and promotions laws generally focus on the end result, the naming of a winner and distribution of prizes, rather than on any information which may be provided to prospective entrants along the way. At the outset, this means that the easiest way to avoid foreign requirements is simply not to let foreign residents enter, and if any do, to disqualify them. Unfortunately, not all aspects of running an online promotion are this simple, and in some cases, you may *want* to open up the promotion to people living outside the United States.

The map you and your entrants will follow, and to which regulators will look to verify your compliance with any applicable laws, will be your official rules. You should contact a qualified legal adviser to lead you through the requirements regarding the text, format, and availability of the rules. It is safe to assume that your rules must be in plain language (understandable by the group to which the promotion is directed), and easily accessible to anyone who wishes to read them. Remember too that you must not grant prizes to anyone who violates your rules and that you (and any promotions manager you hire) must comply in full as well with any obligations placed upon you within the text of the rules.

To accomplish whatever goals you have for an online promotion, or to decide if you want to run one at all, the best tactic is to take a page from journalism and break down your inquiry into the five Ws and H: who, what, when, where, why, and how. Planning an online prize promotion requires a somewhat different order for the questions:

◆ **Who** makes up the targeted group for this promotion?
◆ **Where** does your intended audience live?
◆ **What** kind of promotion do you want to run?
◆ **Why** do you want to run a prize promotion as opposed to other kinds of site or brand publicity?
◆ **When** do you need to start and finish the promotion?
◆ **How** will you handle management of the promotion, including any problems that may arise?

Who: Choosing the Target for Your Giveaway

ANY PROMOTION MUST HAVE AN INTENDED DEMOGRAPHIC, geographic, or economic audience. On the Internet, the prospective choices are much broader than for traditional media, because of the increased reach. Unlike a few years ago when the vast majority of Internet users were college students or young professional scientists, today's Internet community spans almost all age brackets from the very youngest (served by sites such as Nickelodeon's NickJr, <http://www.nickjr.com>, and the Children's Television Workshop, <http://www.ctw.org>) to the "senior circuit" (who may go to any of the tens of sites indexed by Yahoo! at <http://dir.yahoo.com/Society_and_Culture/Cultures_and_Groups/Seniors/>).

The ability to "slice and dice" likely demographics for an online promotion is one of the ways that the Internet surpasses traditional media. Before the Web, only the most profitable demographics got targeted materials, with others ignored or marginalized.

Unfortunately, marketing to certain communities of users, particularly those under age 18, brings a broader set of laws and regulations (the issues regarding marketing to children will be explored later in this chapter). Promotion targeting one economic or racial group may unintentionally and illegally exclude another, whether explicitly or by implication, and subject a business to equal-protection laws. Even senior citizens, presumed to be the most experienced customers, have been the subject of enforcement actions following promotions in traditional media. One example involved the "You May Have Already Won $1,000,000!"-type mailings enticing seniors to fly to contest headquarters on the mistaken impression that they had in fact won. Seniors are also unfortunately often the target of fraudulent sweepstakes and promotions designed to steal from them, another impetus to create senior-focused promotional regulation and advisories. The National Fraud Information Center at <http://www.fraud.org/elderfraud/elderfraud.htm> publishes some helpful information on this topic.

The Internet cannot identify the user to whom a promotion is shown, because the contact between the company and the recipient of the promotion is almost entirely anonymous. Although a contest mailing may use a third-party database or purchased mailing list to limit recipients to the desired audience, a giveaway on a Web site is open to anyone with a Web browser, and the user may falsely state his or her age. By the time an advertiser verifies the age of a sweepstakes winner prior to issuing a prize, it may have already violated the rules for promotions.

Because age-related rules for promotions often deal with the presentation rather than the distribution of prizes, there may be no way for you to entirely eliminate the possibility that an online promotion will violate the law. Instead, concentrate on these strategies to reduce any risk based on targeting an age group:

◆ Tailor the methods by which you publicize your promotion (traditional print and broadcast ads, announcements on products, banner ads on other sites, and/or direct mail) by the likely audience for those media. That way, it's more likely that a desired audience member will receive notice of your contest, while others will never hear about it.

◆ Make sure your instructions, disclaimers, and other promotion materials make it obvious to all potential entrants at whom you are targeting the promotion, the actual chance of winning, and any age restrictions.

- Take a look at other promotions aimed at the same target audience; observe their language and disclaimers (although don't assume that they are necessarily correct in their approach!).
- If your entry form is online, add an age category, and set your site to reject or verify any age which is outside your desired limitations.
- Make it clear in your official rules that entrants below a certain age either may not enter, or must have an adult enter on their behalf, and that all winners' ages will be verified by affidavit—then make sure you follow through on this requirement.
- Familiarize yourself with and avoid at least the basic, most blatant audience-related mistakes made in promotions, such as misstatement or concealment of actual odds.

Where: the Regional Issues of Promotions

AN ADVERTISER MAY DESIRE TO TARGET A PROMOTION AT residents of multiple or even hundreds of countries, especially if the advertiser is a global marketer with recognizable brand equity. On the other hand, many companies have little or no interest in selling product or building a brand name overseas. Companies may also wish to avoid the liability which comes from targeting promotions to foreign countries, or may want to avoid the expense of a full international legal review. What can these companies do to run a promotion only for their target audience?

The first tactic is to list those countries or regions where you would like to offer the promotion. These may be current or future markets or locations of affiliates. Next, find specialized advisers (either attorneys or promotions companies) with the resources to evaluate the legality of your promotion in those markets. Some advisers will charge you a fixed fee per region, others an hourly rate for the research—be sure to get an estimated price in advance. You may find that the cost of a complete research project is prohibitive; if so, begin cutting down your list of preferred regions to those with the highest priority for your marketing efforts. Finally, once you have a clear sense of the requirements for

The Sun Java Cup International— A Challenge of Global Proportions

WHEN SUN MICROSYSTEMS first launched its Java programming language as the optimal underpinings for many World Wide Web sites, it sought to encourage Java development by sponsoring a contest entitled the Java Cup International for the best "applets" (Sun's name for Java programs running within Web sites). The managers in charge of the project initially wanted to open up the contest to everyone in the world, since Internet development was happening everywhere, and Sun already had a multinational presence. Immediately, though, the company ran into a legal brick wall: the cost of researching and complying with the hundreds of applicable laws was staggering, and it was not even clear whether Sun could meet all of the requirements even if it wanted to.

Sun's Alexandre Valais says in the *Java World* online magazine (<http://www.javaworld.com/javaworld/jw-08-1996/jw-08-javacup.html>) that in the end, the contest's administrators limited the entrants to forty-one countries. They excluded users under 18 and those from places like Italy, whose "upfront tax of one-third the total prize amount" would have been prohibitive, since the total prize distribution was international. Java awarded its prizes at the first JavaOne conference in May 1996.

Sun's official rules included the following disclaimer language:

"Open to residents, of legal majority age or older, of your promotion, ensure that you have sufficient lead time to comply with any advance obligations and assign any necessary reporting or other follow-up tasks for the conclusion of the promotion. Make sure as well to document and maintain records of your compliance efforts, in the event a regu-

Argentina, Australia, Austria, Belgium, Brazil, Bulgaria, Canada (except Quebec), Chile, Colombia, Croatia, Czech Republic, Denmark, Egypt, Finland, Germany, Greece, Hong Kong, Hungary, Ireland, Israel, Japan, Korea, Malaysia, Mexico, the Netherlands, New Zealand, Norway, the Republic of the Philippines, Poland, Portugal, Romania, Russia, Singapore, South Africa, Spain, Sweden, Switzerland, Taiwan, Turkey, United Kingdom, and the United States (except Vermont), who have Internet access as of November 30, 1995, with the exception of any employees or contractors of Sun Microsystems, Inc., Netscape Communications Corporation, Oracle Corporation, or J. Brown/ LMC Group, (or employees or contractors of their respective affiliates, subsidiaries or agencies), the judging panel, the immediate families of such employees or contractors and the judging panel, together with those with whom such persons are domiciled, and government employees associated with procurement (US, international, state and local), unless otherwise authorised [sic] under the laws of the jurisdiction concerned. Entries may be submitted on an individual entrant basis ("individual" defined as a natural person), or on a group or team basis, in which case the registration and submission will identify a leader of such group or team. Corporate entities are not eligible."
<http://java.sun.com/applets/archive/javacontest/rules/, accessed November 1, 1998>

lator should challenge your diligence.

Don't think, though, that the "where" question deals only with international legal regime. Even within the United States, there isn't uniformity among the regulations controlling promotions. Florida is among the most notorious for creating difficulties, with advance registration and bonding requirements, and strict rulings about issues such as whether online promotions must have postcard entry in order to be legal (see Department of Licensing of Florida's Department of State: <http://licgweb.dos.state.fl.us/promotions/index.html>). New York and Rhode Island also have bonding requirements, although less stringent than those of Florida. Other states have rules prohibiting or limiting contests (as opposed to sweepstakes) or what kind of payment to or significant effort from entrants is permissible.

What: Types of Promotions

ALTHOUGH MANY BUSINESSPEOPLE USE THE TERMS *CONTEST, sweepstakes,* and *giveaway* interchangeably, they are not identical. Actually, the differences among these types of promotions are substantive and greatly affect the legality and management of your promotion.

How can you tell whether a particular promotion will be considered a permissible sweepstakes or contest versus an often-illegal lottery? At the most basic, the definitions come down to two questions: what must people do to enter, and what must they do to win? Each of the three common types of promotions has a different set of answers to these two questions:

1 **Sweepstakes.** The simplest definition for a *sweepstakes* is "game of chance." In other words, the choice of a winner is entirely random—no skills or payment by the winner are required. Entrants for most sweepstakes is "not just purchasers." Although you may limit by age or geography, you may not, under most states' promotions laws, require someone to buy a product before being eligible to win a prize. Doing so runs the risk of being considered a lottery (see below).

2 **Contest.** For a promotion to be considered a *contest*, it must include some element of skill. The skill need not be advanced; some contests merely ask the entrants to fill in answers to questions readily found on packages or Web sites, or to complete other basic tasks. Keep in mind, though, that

from the point of view of regulators, time truly is money. An overly ambitious set of tasks for entrants may be defined under the law as requiring payment equivalents. Games of skill, as opposed to games of chance, may have more stringent licensing and bonding requirements, and if your contest will require judging, you must ensure that the criteria by which you state entrants will be judged are actually applied. In some situations, a promotion may have elements of both sweepstakes and contests (e.g., "winner will be picked at random from all entrants with the correct answers"). In such a case, the more stringent contest regulations will be applied, regardless of the random aspect of the award.

3 Lottery. More than just a scratch-off or number-drawing run by a governmental agency, *lottery* in its broadest meaning refers to any promotion requiring payment to enter. Money, proof of purchase of goods or services, significant effort, or even service or membership fees required prior to entry may all be considered payment for legal purposes. Most states prohibit private lotteries, which is why even promotions that are seemingly completely tied to products (e.g., scratch-off games at McDonald's or the local gas station) will have nonpurchase entry options. Even newspaper promotions having winning information in the daily or Sunday paper will usually contain a statement, "newspaper can be read at local library."

Promotions on the Internet, though, have repeatedly raised an interesting and important question: is the cost of online access sufficiently high to turn any sweepstakes or contest into a lottery? In other media such as postal or telephone entries the prevailing opinion is that the cost of a stamp or a telephone call is so nominal that it does not cross over the line into a payment. Consider, though, that access to the Internet for most people requires subscribing to an account with an Internet service provider; buying a modem-equipped or otherwise networked computer, or at the very least, a WebTV terminal, or having an employer or school purchase one on their behalf; and licensing software for that machine. According to this argument, having an Internet-only entry method is as if stamps could only be purchased in $1,000 bundles, or telephone sweepstakes could only be entered via cellular telephones.

Most authorities have taken the position that the cost for a particular Internet sweepstakes entry does not rise to the level of payment, and that therefore such a promotion would not be considered a lottery. To the extent that a state or other relevant jurisdiction does rule that online-only promotions require too much of an investment, most will still permit the promotion provided that an offline entry method (e.g., via a postcard) is available. From a business perspective, having to track incoming postcards (versus operating a Web site and storing entries in a database) adds significantly to the cost of managing a promotion. On the other hand, not complying with applicable law can certainly be even more costly, and the vast majority of entrants will usually come through via a Web site anyway.

Most companies ultimately choose either a sweepstakes or contest and then craft official rules to obey the law. Of course, the determination is not definitive—the regulators have a say as well, and disputing their judgment requires time, money, and sometimes, litigation. As a result, unless there is a particular commercial reason not to do it, your easiest approach is to formally exclude residents of a troublesome jurisdiction from entering or winning the promotion.

Why Run an Online Sweepstakes or Contest?

FROM THE ANSWERS TO OUR "WHO," "WHERE," AND "WHAT" questions, you can see that running an online promotion may be much more complicated than you first thought. Why, then, should you bother? Many would argue that many other methods of promoting a site are simpler, less costly, and perhaps just as effective for driving traffic. Even advertising, which is itself the subject of a great deal of regulation, is easier to manage than a sweepstakes or contest. Still, there are literally thousands of prize promotions running on the Web and in e-mail every day, and although a good number of those are done in disregard or outright violation of applicable law, many (particularly those run by larger, more established companies) are fully qualified and legal, meaning that someone in management thought it worth the time and effort.

One answer to the "why" question is that prize promotions have features unavailable in almost any other kind of promotion:

◆ **User data.** With a prize promotion such as a sweepstakes, you will get at least some demographic and personal information from your entrants. After all, you need to be able to notify them and/or send them their prizes if they win, so it's in their best interest to provide the requested data to you. Users normally hesitant to answer questions about their age, address, or economic status will give promotions operators information as a matter of course.

◆ **Repeated contact.** The goal with online promotion is to communicate as often as possible with your users in a way that will not annoy them. One advantage to a prize promotion is that it gives you an excuse for repeated e-mails to your entrants. You can confirm their initial entry, remind them of upcoming deadlines if the promotion allows or requires multiple submissions, name the winner/s, congratulate the winner/s, commiserate with the losers, and offer an advance look at your next promotion. All of these are legitimate messages in the interest of participants in the promotion. Once you're in their e-mail boxes with your contest or sweepstakes mail, there's nothing stopping you from including some additional sales or marketing information, adding to the value of the message to both you and your users.

◆ **Sharing the burden.** Although not unique in this regard, prize promotions are among the easiest ways of splitting marketing costs, even among dissimilar companies. A great number of promotions will have two or more sponsors, each with certain financial and promotional responsibilities for the event but with each also benefiting from the efforts of its partners. Because promotions are so separate from the day-to-day business of most companies, setting up these temporary alliances is much easier through the aid of an online promotions firm such as Yoyodyne Entertainment (now a subsidiary of Yahoo!), which can design and market the entire promotion on behalf of its sponsors. Internet technology also makes it simpler to share information and collateral material for the promotion than is possible in traditional media, such as clickable banners leading to the entry page.

◆ **Creative brand building.** Many companies will establish prizes that, in their own right, serve to build the company's brand. For example, if you are running a sweepstakes with a car or trip as first prize, second or third prize can be t-shirts, hats, or other items bearing your company's logo. By sending them out as prizes, you not only give more people the joy of winning something, but you make it much more likely that they will wear your brand in public than if you made the items available for free—everyone values a prize more than a mass-distributed item. When appropriate, companies can use their own products as prizes.

◆ **Excitement.** The possibility of winning generates enthusiasm—it's human nature. By promoting your brand or product with a competitive promotion, you can build positive associations for your customers, which can translate into increased sales later on.

When Will the Promotion Occur?

ONE KEY DIFFERENCE BETWEEN A PRIZE PROMOTION AND a traditional ad is that the timing is a bit more complicated for a promotion. An Internet promotion can be even more of a challenge. A company must make sure that an advertisement runs during the targeted period, and that consumers have enough time after receiving the ad's message to act on it (as, for example, when you announce a one-day sale on a radio ad). Even if an advertisement is keyed to a particular product launch, it is fairly simple to choose run dates in advance, provide the ad, and let it happen.

Not so with prize promotions. In addition to the planning of the promotion and any necessary legal review, you must also allow enough time for publicity, a reasonable entry period, processing time for the entries, selection of the winners, verification of the information provided by the winners to ensure their qualification for the prizes (generally done through affidavits of eligibility), obtaining the prizes, announcement of winners, and awarding of the prizes. For online promotions, you may also have to figure in time for any necessary technical development of fraud-resistant, fair, and accurate contest or sweepstakes entry mechanisms with links to a database of entrants. The timing question is also crucial for obtaining approval from regulators. Florida, for example, requires advance notice and registration prior to the opening date of the promotion, and failure to comply may jeopardize your chances of doing a legal promotion in Florida in the future.

How to Manage Prize Promotions

WHAT ARE THE REMAINING ISSUES YOU NEED TO CONSIDER before and during your prize promotion?

♦ Who within your company will be charged with either direct-ly managing the promotion, or coordinating with and over-seeing the outside company you choose to run it? You may want your marketing executives to handle this, since they are probably most familiar with the goals for this promotion and how it fits into your overall advertising effort. They, though, may not be as familiar with the technological and interna-tional issues. Make sure, then, that they have access to and can work with a technically savvy person or team. The tech folks will review the promotion mechanism for online secu-rity concerns (you don't want people automating entries or falsifying identities to increase their chances of winning), evaluate the reliability of the online provider chosen to host the promotion, coordinate any database integration (to track entrants, identify winners), and even explain the Internet to the regulators who may not understand how your promotion will be publicized and operated. Together, the marketing and technical specialists should be able to handle most or all of the questions and problems that arise internally.

♦ What about user questions or complaints, or regulatory enforcement efforts? In an area as heavily regulated as prize promotions, with the type of interest giveaways always gen-erate, you should expect some glitches along the way. It could be as simple as a prospective entrant who can't figure out the Web site or as complicated (and potentially expensive) as a typo in your rules which entitles every entrant to the $100,000 grand prize. Since there's no way to absolutely prevent these types of occurrences, some contingency planning is essential.

1 Make sure all documentation and correspondence is not only kept, but is also easily accessible.

2 Remember that the larger your company, the more likely a regulator will seek to impose liability. Have counsel knowledgeable in advertising and promotions laws review your original promotion rules and procedures, and get them involved early on in any dispute (since they may have dealt with the regulator before).

3 Take a look at your business liability insurance policy to see what it provides for promotional liability, and put an appropriate insurance and indemnification requirement in any contract you sign with a third-party promotions manager.

4 If a mistake or misunderstanding in your rules or promotion causes any public controversy, monitor online discussions to catch any dissent and remember that the Web site you used to run the promotion is a great forum for addressing any common concerns among your users. For example, in the Sun Microsystems Java Cup International contest discussed above, many prospective entrants complained in Usenet newsgroups and elsewhere about the statement that Sun would own all entries outright, worrying that they would be doing free development work for Sun Microsystems to exploit. When Sun learned of the controversy, it quickly posted messages on Usenet and a clarification to the rules on its Web site explaining that the intention in having authors give up their intellectual property rights was to ensure that the winning applications could be freely used by everyone in the public domain, rather than resold or licensed at a profit by Sun.

EYES ON THE PRIZE

OBVIOUSLY, MANY OF THE SWEEPSTAKES AND CONTESTS BEING run on the Internet have not complied with all of the requirements and techniques discussed here. These guidelines, though, will help you not only to run your own prize promotion, but also to evaluate whether you want to be involved in another company's promotion, and what your potential exposure might be. One more recommendation: enter a few of the online promotions yourself to see how they work and where they might lack either usability or legality. Not only is this useful research...but hey, you might even win something at the same time!

MARKETING TO THE WORLD?

THIS BOOK DISCUSSES THE INTERNATIONAL SCOPE OF THE Internet and how it affects issues such as advertising regulation, online business, and promotions. In many cases, a site owner may not intend or desire to target a worldwide audience with its site, and must take steps to avoid or minimize cross-border contact. As we have seen, disclaimers, verification, research, and even insurance are all elements of the risk-management strategy.

If you *want* to reach foreign as well as domestic customers, however, the Internet is the cheapest and fastest way to go. Here are a few of the many examples of businesses wanting to encircle the globe:

◆ **Multinational marketers**, particularly those with a single set of products and/or services, or those businesses that service multinational companies
◆ **Online communities of interest**, whose success depends on numbers of users with similar interests rather than geographic exclusivity
◆ **Mail-order retailers**, especially of goods that are rarely subject to tariffs, who are able to ship overseas
◆ **News, information, and entertainment sites**
◆ **Tourism and local information sites catering to foreign visitors**

With all of these groups, it is critical to "get it right the first time," to ensure that the Web site and the supporting mechanisms for the business work well together to serve the user halfway around the world as well as the one halfway down the block.

Of course, companies have been marketing around the world for years, via television, print publications, and other means, but they've usually done so after careful investigation, or in stages. Web-based businesses, though, rarely have or take the time to do this kind of analysis. Not being able to limit the countries receiving their Web site can have unintended and unpleasant consequences, since the same instantaneous communication which shoots their messages to their prospective customers can also circulate user complaints about poor service or faulty goods. Even miscommunications between you and your customers can generate mounds of bad publicity, because it's difficult for you to recover from a concentrated word-of-Internet bad report. You can never recall all the negative postings and can never know when they'll show up on a search engine result for your business.

The process of internationalizing a business is a broad-based task which can involve all aspects of your business. There are a few Internet-specific or at least Internet-intensified risks that are worth focusing on:

- ◆ Translation of your content
- ◆ Fulfillment and customer service for orders
- ◆ Differences in access speed and technology available to users
- ◆ Intellectual property protection under different legal systems

The Requirements and Risks of Translating and Localizing a Web Site

THE INTERNET BEGAN AS AN ENGLISH-ONLY SYSTEM, NOT JUST because of its origins in the U.S. Department of Defense, but also because most computers supported only ASCII characters. ASCII stands for American Standard Code for Information Interchange, indicating its English-speaking origins. It contained limited or no support for diacritical marks and none for other language alphabets within its 128 characters. At the time, anyone attempting to transmit to speakers of Japanese, Hebrew, Cyrillic, or any other non-Latin-character language would have to resort to a combination of transliteration and translation to get the message across. Happily for the non-English speaking world, the 'Net's technology and culture have grown beyond this limitation, and today online resources are available in tens of different languages.

Not all users can even access each of those languages, however, let alone understand them. While the standard Internet access software such as Netscape Navigator and Microsoft's Internet Explorer supports multiple character sets, often the user needs to have additionally installed system extensions or at least appropriate fonts to read non-English Web sites. If not, the site will often come up as gibberish or boxes surrounding nonsense characters. With the right software and supporting files installed, though, it's as if the user were given a personal Rosetta Stone—suddenly, everything becomes legible and usable.

From a site design perspective, you may wish to have your site available in a foreign language or more than one language simultaneously, depending on your chosen audience. It's a great feature, but also one fraught with business and legal risks.

One attractive option when internationalizing a Web site is either to contract with a translation service, or (much less expensively) obtain some of the newer software packages that claim to translate content. The first thing to be aware of is that any software-driven translation will likely not be of business-critical quality—language simply has too many idioms and too much nuance for the successful translation of all but the most simple words and phrases. For speakers of foreign languages, the easiest way to verify this is to type an English phrase into an online translation engine such as the Babelfish service run by Altavista in conjunction with Systran Translation Software (found at <http://babelfish.altavista.com>), select translation into the other language you speak, and click "Translate." As good as the underlying software may be, it's likely that at least some of the translated words or phrases will be incorrect. Further, if you tell the site to translate back into English, any errors will be compounded (like a multilingual game of "Telephone"), and by the third or fourth back-and-forth iteration the phrase will be unrecognizable. *(See "The Babel Fish Out of Water".)*

Even manual translation services may pose problems for your business. First, the translators may not have sufficient knowledge of the language and relevant cultural issues for the project, and if you yourself do not have employees with such familiarity, you may not be aware of the problems until after the site is launched. Unfortunately, this is not something you can easily prevent via negotiation or preagreement; it is difficult to specify language ability or cultural sophistication requirements within a contract, so you may not even be able to get written assurance of the needed skills. Second, even if the translators are generally fluent in the relevant languages, they may not be familiar with the specialized vocabulary used by your company and its customers, and may therefore mistranslate less-common

The Babel Fish Out of Water

IN DOUGLAS ADAMS'S *Hitchhiker's Guide to the Galaxy,* the galactic travelers were able to get around interspecies language problems with the aid of an amazing creature known as the Babel fish. As the eponymous guide states in one particularly bizarre passage:

The Babel fish...is small, yellow and leechlike, and probably the oddest thing in the Universe. It feeds on brainwave energy received not from its own carrier but from those around it. It absorbs all unconscious mental frequencies from this brainwave energy to nourish itself with. It then excretes into the mind of [the] carrier a telepathic matrix formed by combining the conscious thought frequencies with nerve signals picked up from the speech centers of the brain which has supplied them. The practical upshot of all this is that if you stick a Babel fish in your ear you can instantly understand anything said to you in any form of language.

SOURCE: *THE HITCHHIKER'S GUIDE TO THE GALAXY* (NEW YORK: POCKET BOOKS, 1979), PP. 59–60.

idiomatic expressions and jargon. If you try to use a single service for multiple languages, you risk uneven translation quality; if you mix and match among multiple services, you can delay your project's conclusion and can also risk inconsistency in understanding.

Once the initial translation is performed and the site is launched, your problems are far from over. You must now ensure that each version of the site is updated on the same schedule and matches the quality of the others, or at least that each follows an appropriate update schedule of its own. Keeping a single site current is difficult—keeping multiple sites up-to-date can overwhelm an unprepared company. The quality control issues for the initial translation are magnified during the update process, because of the likelihood that one or more of the other companies on which you depend will be out of business, unavailable, or otherwise unable to provide updates on a timely basis. You may have to begin the search for appropriate translation personnel once again.

In the end, all you can do is work carefully with the chosen translation service or services to minimize any possible problems, get references for each service relevant to your specific industry, and allow sufficient lead time so that if problems do develop and the service is unable to complete its work, you will have time to substitute other translators prior to site launch. It always pays to identify a few different vendors, in case one is unavailable for the initial work or any update, and to ensure you have often-refreshed copies of the translators' work and source material in case you need to make a quick switch. It's also good practice to have a network of native speakers of each of the chosen languages who will spot-check the translations for accuracy, idiom, and typographical errors. Finally, just as you would limit eligibility in a prize promotion to those regions most important to your business to save on regulatory burdens and costs, so too should you think carefully about your business needs before electing to translate your site into another language.

The Foreign Customer
Service Quandary

BECAUSE INTERNET USERS ALL OVER THE WORLD CAN COM-
municate, compare notes, and complain about your company, it is imperative to provide equivalent (if not identical)
delivery and customer support options in each region to
which you will be providing goods or services. If you are
unable to do so and cannot give an acceptable explanation
for the differences to those customers who receive less-than-
par service, you may find yourself losing sales not only in
those regions but also in others as your reputation is tar-
nished. Avoiding negative consumer opinion is critical.

How can you assure appropriate levels of service and support and manage customer expectations, particularly if you
are a small company with no other international offices or
operations, using only the Internet as your conduit to the
world? Your first and most expensive option is to establish
foreign offices. For particularly personnel-intensive or profitable foreign businesses, it's certainly worth the cost and
time required. Many companies, though, will have to look
into other options.

One possibility is to contract with a local service provider
in each target country to act as your representative in dealing
with your customers' requests. You may select a firm specializing as a local servicer or a shipping company with an affiliated business services offering, or identify a company with
appropriate skills and location and create a customized relationship. In either case, you will have to work out a number
of crucial details to make the subcontracting work:

◆ **Quality control.** How can you ensure that your foreign-ser-
vice partner will meet your company's quality and customer
relationship standards? Certainly, such standards should be
spelled out as explicitly as possible within the contract you
sign. The agreement should also grant you inspection rights,
regular reports (including any complaints and the steps
taken to correct them), and a process for resolving disputes
and/or terminating the relationship.

◆ **Sharing data.** You will need a mechanism for sharing data on customer identity, warranty entitlement, specific configuration, and any required payments. This sharing may take place online via synchronized databases or via faxed or mailed documentation. The agreement should specify the types and the format of information being shared and how errors will be corrected.

◆ **Branding.** How (if at all) will your foreign servicers display your brand in public? What consequences may result from their indiscriminate use of your trademarks and good will? You should keep in mind that your trademarks may not have the same level of protection overseas, and might even infringe on a foreign country's registered marks, so it's best to include appropriate research responsibility in your relationship.

◆ **Parts and inventory.** Will you need to supply the contractor with replacement parts and new inventory, or is there a local supplier of sufficient quality to keep costs low? With what import/export regulations might you have to comply if you are sending materials abroad?

◆ **Noncompetition.** How can you prevent your foreign service provider from taking your customers and sales information and using them to compete with you at a lower price in its country? What about protecting your confidential information from disclosure? Make sure your contract includes appropriate protection for your company.

One final alternative is somewhat of a compromise between subcontracting and establishing your own local presence in your target countries: acquiring foreign companies as subsidiaries to expand your operations overseas. Depending on your specific financial and operational requirements, this can make a great deal of sense. It provides much greater quality and informational control than a subcontractor relationship does, and it can be used as a launching point for many other business opportunities beyond simple customer service. When compared with starting an office from scratch, buying an existing business provides staff, local contacts, and the very real benefit that the many difficult but necessary start-up problems have already been dealt with. On the other hand, depending on the availability of existing businesses and the complexities of the deal, an acquisition can be a major endeavor. Failing to close the deal for whatever reason may put you back to square one without a local presence to show for it.

Beyond these considerations, whether and how you go about establishing a local presence in another country will be driven by your customers' expectations. What levels of technical or sales support are common in their country? How much help are they likely to need with your particular product or service? For that matter, how onerous is the local consumer protection law, and are you required to provide specific customer service or to designate a local agent? The answers to questions such as these will guide you as you establish an international Internet-based business.

Planning for Different Access Routes

USERS IN THE UNITED STATES MAY HAVE DIFFERENT-SPEED modems and different computer platforms for which a site owner needs to plan, but the international audience has even more diversity in technology and Web-access cost. Users may be coming in via teletext terminals, ten-year-old PCs, or a workstation running the latest Unix variant, and their telephone access may be fiber optic or party line. Worse still, whatever the hardware limitations, the cost of online access can be sharply different, with some users paying high per-minute fees even for local calls or having to dial out of their countries just to get an ISP carrier tone. Foreign governments may also monitor or censor online content, slowing down the process further.

How can you plan for the variety of different access issues your users will face as you try to attract international attention for your site? The simplest answer is to work toward the lowest common denominator—a text-based site friendly even to a Lynx browser (advantageous to visually-impaired users as well as low-bandwidth ones), with small per-page file sizes and no plug-in browser extensions required. On the other hand, such a bare-bones site may not fulfill your marketing or feature objectives, since the simpler browsers may not correctly handle cookies (see page 162), SSL encryption, or the other tools available for personalizing and enhancing a site. You therefore want to strike a balance among these different considerations:

- ◆ **Create variations of your sites.** You can use text-only, light graphics, or heavy graphics, which either are user-selected or automatically offered based upon the type of browser software. Keep in mind that for sites which are made up of static HTML pages (as opposed to automatically generated from databases of content), multiple versions will have the same update issues and problems as do multiple language versions of a site. Remember to test your site over time with different types of computers and modems to verify that it continues to be current and accessible to all levels of users.

- ◆ **Offer alternative delivery methods for content.** To the extent that users may find it easier to receive information from your site via e-mail, fax, or download, make these options conveniently available. This need not cost you much more than the HTML versions—even faxing can be inexpensive if done via local mirrored fax server computers.

- ◆ **Avoid too many tricks.** Even if you wish to make your site fancier, do so via standard HTML and a smaller and more universal color palette instead of with Javascript, Java, or style sheets that may differ among browsers. Your site need not be entirely a lowest-common-denominator effort, but certain of its elements can go that route without overly impeding your creativity.

- ◆ **Solicit and react to usability comments from your audience.** You can't predict all the ways people may access your site, but you can continually improve its appeal based upon what your users tell you about their access experience.

It's a safe bet that problems will lessen as time goes by as higher-level technology expands from the larger, industrialized nations across the world. In the meantime, showing sensitivity to your users' efforts to get online and actually view your site will generate appreciation and loyalty. Remember, too, one added benefit of reducing the bandwidth needed to view your site—those users who do have high-speed computers and connections will experience your site in hyperspeed, making it more appealing to them as well.

International Intellectual Property Challenges for Online Businesses

THE TERM *INTELLECTUAL PROPERTY* CAN BE DEFINED AS those intangibles which can be owned and controlled by a business. Most people, however, think of three broad categories when thinking about intellectual property protection: copyright, trademark, and patent. Intellectual property questions are integral to the use of the Web—after all, everything on the Web is in some way or another intellectual property (general issues relating to copyright and trademark are discussed in detail in Chapter 1).

What are the additional international concerns which are raised by putting your company's intellectual property, or using someone else's, on the Internet? We have previously addressed some of them, such as accidental breaches of territorial licenses. The protection issue, though, is of particular concern, because there are almost no technological methods for preventing someone from copying the content of your Web site. Because every Web site actually sends copies of its content to everyone viewing the site, all the users need to do is to save the files to disk. Of course, any site will have difficulty detecting and opposing these kinds of unlawful infringements, no matter where they occur. The frightening thing is that, depending on the intellectual property laws of the jurisdiction where the copying takes place, it may in fact not be illegal, even if you explicitly prohibit copying of your content in the text of your site. Even worse, you may not have the protection you believe you do, or you could even be infringing on someone else's rights in that jurisdiction.

Although copyright and patent are the subject of significant international standardization, trademark is local in both its protection and its limitations, and other countries' trademark registrations can significantly overlap with those of the United States. Alternatively, the copying may be illegal, but you have no legal means of bringing the culprit to court, because you are not local and may not have the right to sue. Less than wholesale commercial counterfeiting would usually not merit extradition, even from countries with which treaties exist.

As with so many of the other areas discussed in this book, the best you can do to protect intellectual property is to create a strategy to identify, reduce, and manage the risk of infringement by someone located outside of your jurisdictional reach:

1 Know what intellectual assets you have placed on your site. Too often, site management is done on an ad hoc basis, with no one having a proper inventory of what's been used to create and update the site. This poses problems when others make infringement claims against you, but it also makes it difficult to manage your own intellectual property and to reduce the possibility of infringements.

2 Don't leave the safe open—choose from your less-valuable intellectual property when building your site. For example, if your company owns particularly famous and valuable graphics or artworks which it uses as part of its corporate identity, you need not put large-sized, clean copies on your site; low-resolution "thumbnails" of the pieces may serve the necessary purpose, while making it more difficult for infringers to get quality material for their misuse.

3 Use intelligent file names and image labels to reduce the likelihood of illicit copying, and make it easier to track files which are incorporated into other Web sites. Include your company's name in the file name under which each of your content elements is saved (e.g., Company124.jpg, Company127.jpg)—if the infringer is careless enough to simply copy the file without changing its name, a search engine like Altavista can look for those file names on any site but yours. Further, make sure you include both invisible digital watermarks and visible indicia of ownership wherever possible in the files (for graphics, this may be onscreen; for sound and video files, it can also be done within the identifying information stored with the file) to make it more difficult for any infringer to argue it did not know the materials were proprietary.

4 Work with foreign counsel to obtain legal protection for your most valuable intellectual property included within your Web site, such as your domain names, trademarks, and the patents on any business processes incorporated into your site. Copyright is less of an issue, since most nations' laws provide for reciprocal rights and instant protection on creation.

5 When choosing the countries for your Internet business, consider where you have sufficient operations or business to justify the expense and assert jurisdiction in the event of a dispute. But, also consider which regions would be targeted by any site copying yours.

REAPING THE BENEFITS OF AN INTERNATIONAL FOCUS FOR YOUR WEB SITE

AFTER ALL THE TRANSLATING, REVISING, LOCALIZING, AND protecting is accomplished, what have you gained? Despite the work entailed in taking all the risk-management steps spelled out, it remains true that the Internet provides the easiest and least expensive way to reach an international audience. From the largest multinational conglomerate to the smallest online storefront, the distance from here to there (no matter where "there" is!) is no longer measured in miles, but in keystrokes and mouseclicks. Further, it's more than likely that as the world economy becomes more interconnected via the Web, the various local governments will be forced to work together on regulatory conformance. International marketing will become a normal and normalized businesses activity.

SPAMMING CUSTOMERS FOR PROFIT AND LOSS

IMAGINE THAT THE POST OFFICE HELD A CLEARANCE SALE: PAY for one letter and mail 10,000 more for free. Not only that, but you could send a twenty-pound package to each person for the same single stamp purchase. As a bonus, you could put random addresses on the packages, and the letter carriers would sort the good addresses from the bad ones, and give you an itemized list. Then imagine the sale had no expiration date. There's no doubt that this would revolutionize the use of the mail for commerce.

Imagine one other scenario: as part of its recycling efforts, your city imposed a per-page charge to recycle your discarded mail. The spate of catalogs arriving during holiday season might end up costing some residents hundreds of dollars in fees. Certainly, any store that decided to mail out a 1,200-page obscure specialty catalog to every city resident would quickly find complaints and even lawsuits arriving from uninterested and impoverished recipients.

What do these two scenarios have in common? They are both fairly accurate analogies for the imagined benefits and actual costs of unsolicited commercial e-mail (UCE) or postings to online discussions, collectively and colloquially known as *spam* (see the sidebar on the following two pages). From the sender's perspective, UCE seems like a no-lose proposition: write a sales solicitation or invitation to visit a Web site, buy a bulk e-mail list or develop a list of Usenet newsgroups, fire up one of the many bulk–e-mail software packages, and press "send." In the time it takes the computer to push the address lists up the line to an Internet-connected server, the message is delivered. Smarter software packages can be set up to track rejected or invalid addresses, making the next mailing that much more efficient.

From a user perspective, the power of spam is not in its convenience but rather its cost, in both time and money. Internet access is rarely free—many people pay directly, others through agreeing to receive advertising with their e-mail, and still others enjoy "free" access paid for by their employers (ostensibly for business purposes). The problem is exacerbated when users must pay telephone or other telecommunications charges in addition to Internet access fees, and when a low-bandwidth connection (such as through an older modem, or a cellular or other wireless carrier) is monopolized by junk e-mail. Additional time and money are spent for systems administrators to delete mail and respond to complaints about unsolicited e-mail. Even worse, damage

First Thing We Do, Let's Kill All the Spammers

CANTER & SIEGEL AND THE "GREEN CARD LOTTERY" SPAM

THE PREVAILING THEORY for the origin of the Internet jargon term *spam* is that it comes from a Monty Python comedy sketch, in which diners at a particular restaurant are offered mainly dishes with varying amounts of Spam luncheon meat within them. "Well, there's egg and bacon; egg, sausage, and bacon; egg and Spam; egg, bacon, and Spam; egg, bacon, sausage, and Spam; Spam, bacon, sausage, and Spam; Spam, egg, Spam, Spam, bacon, and Spam; Spam, sausage, Spam, Spam, Spam, bacon, Spam, tomato and Spam...." From this routine, the term became synonymous with unsolicited messages sent to large numbers of people, or to multiple, off-topic newsgroups.

One of the first and largest of the Internet spammings, which used Usenet rather than e-mail, was perpetrated by two Arizona immigration lawyers, Lawrence Canter and Martha Siegel. On April 14, 1994, readers of approximately 6,000 of the then-10,000 or so Usenet newsgroups saw a message entitled "Green Card Lottery!" The article, which solicited legal clients for Canter and Siegel in connection with an upcoming U.S. government lottery for legal immigrant credentials, was not posted only to applicable topics. Instead, newsgroups from alt.comics.superman to comp.sys.pc.printers to rec.models.railroad all saw the unwanted message appear. What's worse, Canter & Siegel formatted their message in such a way that, rather than a single copy being stored on systems carrying the Usenet feed and showing up in each newsgroup, one copy for every newsgroup was created. In other words, 6,000 separate files appeared on each server computer as the result of a single posting by Canter & Siegel.

The resulting uproar from the Internet community included mass e-mail "bombings" of the attorneys' Internet service provider, bombarding their offices with angry faxes and telephone calls, and online tracking of the two attorneys each time they were forced to switch ISPs after yet another mass posting. Although the two unrepentant lawyers started a company called Cybersell and wrote a book hyping their methods, in fact their efforts generated nothing but ire among most Internet users, and Lawrence Canter was subsequently disbarred by the state of Tennessee for unethical business practices. In the aftermath of the Green Card Lottery spam and other similar efforts, a number of technically savvy Usenet administrators began an ongoing dialogue about techniques for blocking unsolicited, off-topic commercial messages posted to multiple newsgroups.

Marketers who used to bombard fax machines with unsolicited advertisements, like Sanford ("Spamford") Wallace, switched to e-mail. He claims to have sent out as many as 25 million pieces of e-mail every day. He eventually got out of that business after fighting repeated lawsuits from overburdened ISPs.

One result of rampant Usenet spamming was Cancelbot, an automated software-based spam detector and eliminator, and a whole series of methods for targeting or blocking the Cancelbot's activities. Information on Canter & Siegel, Sanford Wallace, and the Cancelbot, along with other spam-related complaints and responses, can be found online in the "Blacklist of Internet Advertisers" at <http://math-www.unipaderborn.de/~axel/BL/blacklist.html>, the "Fight Spam on the Internet" site at <http://spam.abuse.net>, and from the Electronic Frontier Foundation at <http://www.eff.org/pub/Global/America-US/Net_culture/Folklore/Spam/>.

from outside complaints may mount if a spammer lists a third party system as a fraudulent return address. If you consider the millions of people all over the world connected to the Internet, and the thousands of computers acting as Usenet servers for those millions, you begin to see that UCE is far from the risk-free gift to business it first appears to be.

Although the most egregious spammers have brought on technological and legal ramifications, even an otherwise-innocent business that chooses UCE as a promotional technique may find itself the target of legislative enforcement and complaints. What are the kind of responses that any UCE-using business can expect, and what can be done to minimize their likelihood and impact? The clearest approach is to separate the different parties that might react to your UCE mailing, figure out what each group's concerns are, and develop a strategy. The three most likely to play a role in your use of UCE are:

1 Users
2 ISPs and their system administrators
3 Legislators

The Impact of UCE

PEOPLE WHO SIGN UP FOR INTERNET-CONNECTED E-MAIL, whether or not they realize it, have opened themselves up to receiving spam, since the interconnectivity of the Internet means that, absent any technological barriers, anyone can send e-mail to any mail box. Users who sign up for one of the more popular free e-mail services may soon discover that the vast majority of messages they receive are not from relatives or colleagues, but are enticements from sex-themed Web sites, tips on hot (and obscure) penny stocks, chain letters promising to "Make Money Fast," and solicitations for purchases of goods. In some cases, users must go through the inconvenience of changing e-mail addresses in order to stop the overflow of spam—and even then, it may just be a matter of time before the spammers discover the new address.

If the user publishes an e-mail address to the world by using it in the header information of a Usenet post, becoming active in a publicly archived electronic mailing list, or placing it on a Web page, the likelihood of being a UCE target increases significantly. In the same way that Web search pages send out automated "bots" to read and index Web pages without human intervention, creators of electronic bulk mailing lists have a growing number of tools available to them to read the vast amount of online information, locate e-mail addresses, check them for basic validity, and add them to a database. This technique has led many knowledgeable Internet users to post their e-mail addresses in formats designed to block indexing while remaining easily understandable to human respondents: for example, author@ clicking<Spamfighter--delete this part to send me mail> through.com. One casually posted e-mail address without these protections can quickly migrate across multiple databases as vendors buy and incorporate each others' lists, rendering the user's efforts ineffective. Unethical bulk e-mailers will use additional techniques for obtaining and verifying e-mail addresses including:

◆ Generating random potential e-mail addresses by attaching mixes of letters and numbers to well-known domains (such as aol.com, ix.netcom.com, juno.com or hotmail.com), and tracking which addresses bounce as invalid and which are apparently received by real users

◆ Telling respondents to reply to a specific address to be removed from the list, but in actuality using any responses as a means of verifying working addresses for future mailings

◆ Employing "address miners" at low wages to search public forums like chat areas or newsgroups and extract any addresses which might be missed by an automated system.

Remember that if you seek to purchase a bulk e-mail list for your business, the vendor may tell you that all addresses have been verified, duplicates removed and checked for willingness to receive UCE, but this is likely not true.

Even name-gathering techniques that seem perfectly honest can cause user ire. One frequent example is when a company collects e-mail addresses from business cards dropped off at a tradeshow, an online general registration form, or correspondence sent directly from users and creates an e-mail list for "interested people" to which commercial announcements are sent. In many cases, users will complain that they are being spammed and seek assistance from system administrators or otherwise complain to the public about the company's tactics. Even though the user originally voluntarily provided the company with an e-mail address, he or she may have forgotten or may have done so not realizing that the address would be used for unsolicited commercial mailings. The company can be caught completely off-guard by a user complaint when the mailing list was generated from voluntary submissions and may not even know from where the particular user's name came in order to explain why the company felt it appropriate to send a commercial message. The sad truth is that whereas some users might have been open to receiving the message and would have followed through with a purchase or appropriate response, their assumption that the message was unsolicited can create hostility toward the sender.

For Usenet newsgroup readers, the unsolicited commercial message situation is both better and worse than for that of e-mail. On the plus side, tools like the Cancelbots and the strong sense of community on many of the topical newsgroups have combined to reduce or strongly respond to the cross-posted spams of a few years ago. On the other hand, the automated methods only work reliably for cross-posts. The only almost-foolproof method of keeping single-group commercial messages off users' screens is for one user to volunteer as a moderator, filtering all postings before they go out to the public. Not only can monitoring be a time-consuming and often thankless job, but even moderators will occasionally allow unsolicited and inappropriate messages in by error. Also, because of the large volume of postings to some popular unmonitored lists, it can be almost impossible for a user to find desired information in the midst of so much unwanted content, further increasing frustration. Keep in mind, too, that not all users believe that cancelbots are entirely positive—although there is some collaboration among the various cancelbot authors to try to keep accidental deletions of appropriate communications to a minimum, accidents can happen. The same program that deletes mass postings can also read and cancel messages on any topic (or by any other person) disliked by the program's author, allowing people with a specific agenda or point of view to use cancelbots to skew online discussions in their favor. As a result, cancelbots are not without controversy, even as they improve the "signal to noise" ratio for many newsgroups.

Given the inconvenience to users associated with unsolicited commercial messages and the anger that abuses of e-mail or Usenet have caused, is there any way that you can use these inexpensive communications tools to reach new customers or prospects without being deluged with complaints, e-mail bombs, or online negative publicity campaigns as a result? Although true unsolicited commercial e-mail to a bulk mailing list should be avoided, there are a few time-tested methods for getting a commercial message out, even to new recipients, with a minimum of disruption:

1 Always provide users with a reliable means of getting off your address list, and try to include simple instructions for this technique with every mailing. Make sure you have someone responsible for receiving and carrying out removal requests.

2 If you are collecting e-mail addresses for future mailings, keep careful records of the source of the address, and refer to it in your message (e.g., "Your e-mail address was recently entered into a form on our Web site with a request for additional information, and here it is!" or "Thanks for visiting our booth at the recent tradeshow. We thought we'd like to provide you with some more information about the products we displayed at the show").

3 Don't just solicit—contribute. If you want to advertise to a Usenet newsgroup or e-mail discussion list, make the advertisement secondary to actually providing appropriate information to the participants of the list or group. This requires a bit of extra work; you must identify appropriate newsgroups and lists where you may be able to contribute, monitor these targets on a regular basis for appropriate opportunities to answer questions, clarify misconceptions about you or your products, or simply add to the ongoing discussions. At the end of the message, you can either include a note that "if

you'd like more information, please e-mail us," or, even less potentially objectionable, prepare a standard "signature" at the bottom of each post which contains a simple description of your company and how to reach you.

4 Sponsor someone else's message or host a discussion list. While Usenet rarely if ever contains sponsorship opportunities, many other online discussions solicit sponsors to defray their maintenance costs or hosts who will provide bandwidth and server space for the discussion in exchange for ongoing promotional credit. If you find the right mailing list and pick up the sponsorship obligation, you may be able to arrange for your advertisement to be mailed tens of times per day to a self-selected, prime demographics audience—and have them appreciate you for it.

5 Consider utilizing "opt-in" rather than "opt-out." "Opt-out" address collection requires the user to take an action (check a box, send a message) to be excluded from future mailings. With "opt-in," the user must request inclusion in order to receive any mailings. Opt-in may generate fewer names, but you can be certain that everyone on your list wants to be there, causing fewer complaints and making the recipients more interested in the messages you send out. (Yoyodyne Entertainment, acquired by Yahoo! in 1998, extends the "opt-in" philosophy to a series of e-mail and Web-based prize promotions it runs on behalf of sponsors, in which users can choose to participate, part of a concept it calls "permission marketing.")

The more sensitive you are to the severe disruption UCE can cause Internet users, the more likely you are to use rather than abuse e-mail and Usenet to get your message across. Although responsible marketers may garner less public attention than the violators, they will also probably achieve greater initial and, more importantly, repeat business from those targeted, willing individuals to whom their marketing information is sent. The alternative, buying bulk e-mail lists or sending multiple off-topic ads to Usenet newsgroups, may appear less expensive initially, but is almost certain to cost your company much more than it has saved in bad will, lost sales, and time-consuming responses to complaints and technological counterattacks.

System Administrators and Spam

IF SPAM IS AN ANNOYANCE TO AVERAGE USERS, IT CAN BE FAR
worse for the system administrators (or *sysadmins*, for short)
who support them. Consider that a single message sent to
1,000 users on a system means that 1,000 copies of the message get stored on the mail server. Most ISPs do not have
unlimited storage capabilities. A thousand copies of *anything*
can put a dent in their available disk space and system speed,
and if multiple copies are sent or multiple spam messages
arrive on the same day, the unwanted messages can actually
affect the performance of the entire network. While the sysadmins are tracking down the cause of the slowdown, complaints begin arriving from many of the 1,000 users who
object to the spam, demanding that the sysadmins help them
locate and punish the offenders. Most of these complaints
may also attach a copy of the spam, multiplying the number
of times it becomes stored on the mail server. At the same
time, there may be tens or hundreds of incorrect addresses
with the system's domain name being sent from the spammer, which must be processed and rejected by the mail server.
All of this work, both on the part of the mail server and the
sysadmins, is generated by one or more unsolicited mass e-
mailings, and is entirely separate from whatever day-to-day
work the sysadmins must do to maintain the system.

The above scenario assumes the sysadmins are working
with the recipients of the UCE. It is a very different story
when one of the system's users transmits spam to other systems. Suddenly, instead of dealing with complaints from
one set of recipients, the sysadmin may be receiving the
entire catalog of irate responses from tens or hundreds of
ISPs, each with multiple unhappy users. Simultaneously, all
the bounced messages with incorrect addresses are returning to the system, and depending on how the outgoing mail
server is configured, these messages may go back and forth
between the origin system and the domains before the system assumes them to be undeliverable. At this point, the
sysadmin may try to suspend the service of the spam-
sender, if sending the messages violated the terms of service

of the system. Most systems' rules do prohibit sending unsolicited commercial e-mail, but the sysadmin must consider the possibility that the user will claim unfair termination and file a lawsuit.

Worse still are the experiences of those sysadmins who are the victims of spammers who alter message headers to indicate a false origin for the UCE they send. For example, it is a fairly trivial matter to put any address, real or fake, as the sender of an e-mail message or Usenet posting. Although careful analysis of the routing information contained in the "headers" of the message will show that it originated from somewhere other than the indicated source, many users either cannot read such header information, or are on systems (such as America Online) which don't include the headers in the delivered e-mail messages. As a result, any complaints about the spam, or vitriolic responses, will go not to the actual sender and sysadmin from which the message originated, but to the unfortunate and innocent parties whose addresses and/or domain names appear in the message.

Unfortunately, most users whose e-mail address is fraudulently used in these types of spam do not have the resources to find or fight the perpetrators. The ISP, though, can be a different story. From a business perspective, falsifying sender information can be proven as fraud, and the damages suffered by an ISP, particularly a smaller one whose business is seriously disrupted, may be large. Sysadmins generally have the technical skills to review the headers and often collaborate with other sysadmins to track down spammers. Once they do, the sysadmins can provide the information to the ISP management, which may well have the ability to bring a costly lawsuit against the spammer and its ISP for damages. Beyond the lawsuits, sysadmins are also cooperating to create spam-filters (such as Procmail) that detect suspicious messages or previous violators and, at the user's option, delete those messages before they reach the individual inbox. (For more information on sysadmin responses, see <http://spam.abuse.net> and the Usenet newsgroups, <news.admin.net-abuse.e-mail> and <news.admin.net-abuse.bulletins>.)

Because a sysadmin/ISP response, being business-to-business and better funded, has more capability to harm your business, it is critical that you do everything you can to avoid eliciting such a response to your advertising. Again, there are a number of methods you can use to work with (rather than against) the ISPs and still make your promotional information available to interested recipients:

1 Before sending out any promotional mailings, particularly mass mailings, check the terms of service for your company's Internet service provider. The ISP could cancel your company's access, seriously impeding your business operations.

2 Before embarking on an e-mail or newsgroup marketing campaign, assign technically adept employees to review the online sysadmin discussions to find out which mail techniques are acceptable, and which practices and practitioners have garnered the most scorn and anger.

3 If an action by your company, your ISP mail, another of the ISP's customers, or someone fraudulently using one of your addresses to send spam generates a sysadmin response (which may include blocking all incoming e-mail from your company or ISP, no matter the subject matter), contact the ISP community, offer reasonable assistance, and otherwise cooperate to regain e-mail sending privileges.

One final thought on being familiar with the ISP/sysadmin approach to Spam—you may need to take advantage of it yourself one day. Imagine that your company's domain name is falsely used by spammers as a return address, leading to vitriolic responses against your company and blocking by ISPs. You will need to take rapid response not only to discover and possibly prosecute the spammer, but also to contact the user community to explain that you were not the actual sender. Being able to work with the ISPs and their sysadmins to track the mail and disseminate a response is a great boost to your fight against address fraud.

Legislative Responses to Spam

WHEN USER COMPLAINTS AND EVEN ISP LAWSUITS FAIL TO stem the tide of spam overwhelming e-mail boxes, victims have increasingly turned to lawmakers to provide additional remedies and prohibitions. It would not be helpful to try to describe the state of the law—national and local legislatures constantly propose new laws, and laws already enacted are ever subject to court challenges and amendments. Beyond that, different communities may disagree on exactly how "unsolicited commercial e-mail" is defined, and even fellow members of a single community (such as users, or legislators, for that matter) may not interpret UCE in the same way, adding to the difficulty of either describing or predicting the state of anti-spam laws.

Generally speaking, though, the statutory responses to UCE break down into a few main types: prohibition on fraud; limitations on the amount and manner of spam transmissions; and requirements to label the messages to clearly indicate their purpose (and, not incidentally, to empower users to automatically filter and delete unwanted commercial mail).

CRIMINAL LIABILITY FOR MISLEADING OR FRAUDULENT SPAM INFORMATION

A NUMBER OF LEGISLATURES, FROM THE STATE OF GEORGIA to the U.S. government, have crafted anti-spam legislation focusing on one of the larger problems associated with UCE—being unable to accurately determine from whom the mail originated. This includes both messages using someone else's e-mail address and/or using a return address without authorization or editing the header so that the return address is entirely invalid as an e-mail address. Although most legitimate businesses would never consider doing such things, particularly since their goal is to increase the communication between customer and company, online-only businesses (particularly in the adult content or multilevel marketing areas) frequently misuse or intentionally alter the e-mail sender information.

Some lawmakers, though, have found it difficult to prohibit misleading or fraudulent addresses while permitting fanciful e-mail addresses (such as author@clickingthrough.com), and these laws, like many others involving the Internet, also suffer from the drafters' misunderstanding of the Internet and how electronic mail differs from its paper cousin. Misappropriate use of another's identity is already illegal, and any new law must supplement that general principle with Internet-specific additions, such as actually requiring a valid e-mail address on each piece of UCE.

LEGISLATING RESTRICTIONS ON SPAMMING

THE MOST BASIC APPROACH TO REGULATING SPAM IS TO either analogize or directly connect spamming to the most-similar business practice already being regulated—sending unsolicited commercial faxes. Many states as well as the federal government have existing civil and criminal penalties for bombarding unwilling recipients with commercial faxes, due to the inconvenience and direct cost to recipients. These existing laws do not absolutely prohibit unsolicited faxing, which would probably be an unconstitutional restraint on commercial speech, but rather define "time, place, and manner" restrictions. For example, in some jurisdictions, a company may only send unsolicited faxes overnight, keeping the recipients' machines free during business hours for more important documents, and may not send more than a certain number of faxes or pages per event.

Some proposed anti-spam legislation takes the simplest route: adding e-mail to the definition of unsolicited commercial communications in the anti-fax laws, or clarifying an existing definition (which may define faxes as digital communications utilizing telephone lines and received by fax machines, whether sent by computer or fax machine on the sending end). The problem with this approach is that, by directly including electronic mail within a telephone-industry law in one statute, the legislature risks unintentionally inviting a court to bring e-mail under other telephone-related laws (such as FCC jurisdiction or communication taxation), where the analogies are much

Declaring Your True Intentions: Labeling E-mail Advertisements

TO GET A SENSE of how vague some labeling requirements can be, consider the "Unsolicited Commercial
Electronic Mail Choice Act of 1997," introduced in the
U.S. Senate by Senator Murkowski of Arkansas on May
21, 1997 (and found online at <http://thomas.loc.gov/
cgi-bin/query/z?c105:S.771:>), which stated in part:
(a) INFORMATION ON ADVERTISEMENT
(1) REQUIREMENT: . . . .[A] person who transmits an
electronic mail message as part of the transmission of
unsolicited commercial electronic mail shall cause to
appear in each electronic mail message transmitted as
part of such transmission the information specified in
paragraph (3).

(2) PLACEMENT

(A) ADVERTISEMENT: The information specified in
subparagraph (A) of paragraph (3) shall appear as the
first word of the subject line of the electronic mail message without any prior text or symbol.

(B) OTHER INFORMATION: The information specified
in subparagraph (B) of that paragraph shall appear
prominently in the body of the message.

(3) COVERED INFORMATION: The following information shall appear in an electronic mail message under
paragraph (1):

less clear. Significant efforts are being made to differentiate
e-mail and the Internet from audio telephone services. Nevertheless, many users already consider the anti-junk fax
laws applicable to unsolicited commercial e-mail, and some
have even sought to enforce these laws.

(A) The term "advertisement".

(B) The name, physical address, electronic mail address, and telephone number of the person who initiates transmission of the message.

(b) ROUTING INFORMATION: All Internet routing information contained within or accompanying an electronic mail message described in subsection shall be valid according to the prevailing standards for Internet protocols.

(c) EFFECTIVE DATE: The requirements in this section shall take effect 30 days after the date of enactment of this Act.

(1) COMMERCIAL ELECTRONIC MAIL: The term "commercial electronic mail" means any electronic mail that—

(A) contains an advertisement for the sale of a product or service;

(B) contains a solicitation for the use of a toll-free telephone number or a telephone number with a 900 prefix the use of which connects the user to a person or service that advertises the sale of or sells a product or service; or

(C) contains a list of one or more Internet sites that contain an advertisement referred to in subparagraph (A) or a solicitation referred to in subparagraph (B language.

LABELING E-MAILED ADVERTISEMENTS

ONE FINAL APPROACH IS WORTH NOTING: SOME LAWMAKERS have sought to require all senders of unsolicited commercial e-mail to clearly label their messages as "Advertisements" (see the sidebar above). This certainly adds to the convenience for recipients, who can visually or automatically scan and eliminate unwanted messages. On the other hand, what constitutes an advertisement? Would a newsletter filled with useful tips and sent to a compiled mailing list fall under the definition? How about press releases, which are generally not considered ads, although they certainly carry promotional weight?

Assessing the Risk/Reward of Unsolicited Commercial E-mail

GIVEN THAT A SINGLE SPAM E-MAIL MESSAGE SENT TO UN-willing recipients may result in an electronic smear campaign, lawsuits from ISPs, and allegations of criminal activity, you should think twice before implementing unsolicited commercial e-mail efforts. For almost any business, a UCE campaign is probably a bad idea—there are too many pitfalls and possibilities of bad feelings or even monetary damages along the way.

On the other hand, with a properly collected list, clear and useful information within the message, legitimate address removal instructions, and a sensitivity to how and when people prefer to get e-mail, the ire generated by a thoughtless spamming of large ISPs or newsgroups can be replaced by customer appreciation, follow-up opportunities, and (with a bit of luck) solid sales growth. Also consider getting involved with some of the trade and user groups devoted to appropriate commercial uses of e-mail and by educating your local and national representatives, not only about the potential abuses, but also the positive uses of the Internet to inform consumers. You can help ensure that the opportunities for responsible electronic marketing will expand in ways which will benefit your company and its bottom line.

PROTECTING PRIVACY
(IF YOU HAVE TO ASK...)

PRIVACY MEANS DIFFERENT THINGS TO DIFFERENT PEOPLE.
Invasion of privacy can be as mundane as the student whose curious eyes wander to a classmate's paper or as sinister as the camera-toting voyeur peering in an unsuspecting person's window. In the business world, issues of privacy usually involve compliance with applicable laws and cultural norms, which can vary from location to location. Privacy on the Internet embodies two major concepts:

◆ Use and disclosure of "personally identifiable information"
◆ Tracking of an individual user's online behavior.

Personally identifiable information consists of any data which, when taken together, can definitively lead to a particular individual. Obviously, information like a name, address, telephone number, or e-mail address, and particularly any combination of these elements, would be considered personally identifiable information, but these are not the exclusive types of information about which you need to be concerned for privacy protection. Consider a user profile of a female, an accountant, with two children (a boy aged seven and a girl aged twelve), who lives in Roanoke, Virginia. With just these facts, an investigator may be able to positively identify the user. For example, someone could call local schools and say: "I am moving to the area and plan on sending my seven-year-old son to your school in the fall. He's very attached to his twelve-year-old sister, and concerned that he'll never get to see her. Do you have any families in the school with similarly aged children with whom I could speak?" Trade associations and other business listing sources could also be used for information: "I'm doing an article on female accountants who have to balance family and business responsibilities. I was wondering whether you could put me in touch with anyone in the Roanoke area who might consent to be interviewed." Remember, too, that personally identifiable information

155

can be gleaned by combining different databases of otherwise anonymous information. Two collections of survey answers, one about occupation and the other about family status, could be linked via a common identifier (such as a Social Security number) for the nameless respondents, leading to the same amount of usable information as in the previous example.

The problem with the collection and distribution of personally identifiable information is that such data can easily be misused or at least used in a way the individual never envisioned or expected. Even governments, which may have

The Saturn™ Extended Family Database

GENERAL MOTORS'S SATURN DIVISION has, from its inception, marketed itself as more consumer-friendly and people-driven than other car manufacturers. From "no-haggle pricing" to annual get-togethers at the company's Spring Hill, Tennessee plant, this image is part of almost every Saturn marketing campaign. When Saturn first launched its Web site <http://www.saturn-cars.com>, the site included a section called the "Extended Family Database." In this area, Saturn owners could type in their names, locations, information about their families and their cars, and their aspirations. All of this was completely optional, and not posted by the company itself, but every posting was fully available to the public. The notion apparently was to allow Saturn drivers to create their own meta-community using the Saturn Web site as a base.

When creating the Extended Family Database, though, Saturn did not post visible warnings about the potential misuse of the information placed within the site. As a result, there were no technical reasons why the database could not be searched and indexed automatically by, for example, a rival car company that access to much of the same information from other sources, can take advantage of personally identifiable information gathered via a company's Web site, since the information may be matched and focused in a way otherwise unavailable to the governmental agencies collecting broadbased data. Unfortunately, history has shown that corrupt governments can utilize personal information to categorize, discriminate against, and intimidate their citizens, making responsible management of this information vital.

If the protection of users' identities is a critical element of personal privacy, so too is the use of information regarding

could then specifically identify drivers, obtain their addresses, and send them solicitations to switch car brands when their leases were near expiration. For that matter, Saturn itself could certainly have mined the database for additional marketing opportunities to its existing customers by gaining more information than was usually volunteered at the time of purchase. There was enough information freely available to allow criminals or stalkers to potentially gain and abuse the trust of an Extended Family member: "Hello, do you have a husband named Bill who drives a 1995 Saturn coupe? Well, I'm afraid he was in a serious accident—you'll have to come to 125 Center Street immediately!"

Although no such case was ever publicly reported, it is noteworthy that Saturn subsequently removed the Extended Family Database from its site. Of course, Saturn was not the only company to provide opportunities for users to post personally identifiable information without informing them of potential risks—many of the Web's most popular sites have discussion lists, chat areas, and similar open forum features without adequate explanation and warnings to consumers.

their online activities. No matter the context, from the text of a private chat to an item purchased in an online mall to the path taken by a user through a Web portal, a site owner can collect a tremendous amount of behavioral data. Sites may offer additional features such as personalization (the site changes based on stated and observed user preferences, so it's more attractive and efficient for each person) or faster repeat purchases in exchange for tracking activity. There are many potential problems, particularly if the information is associated with other information available about the user (such as a name and address) and used for marketing or more malicious purposes.

Both governments and industry associations have spent a great deal of time trying to come up with rules and policies for the management of private information in cyberspace. Some of these rules, dating back to the pre-Internet period, are concerned with local collection of information and very much driven by the cultural and legal expectations of the particular country. The U.K. Data Protection Act, which places sharp limitations on the types and amount of personal information that can be collected and kept, mandates registration with the government by anyone compiling such data, and requires users to have access to their information. (An official copy of the Data Protection Act can be found on the Web at <http://www.hmso.gov. uk/acts/acts1984/1984035.htm>.) The world remembers governments such as that of Nazi Germany, which used personal information to subjugate the populace. The European Community has followed the model of the U.K. and other member states in establishing its overall privacy principles and rules (<http://www2.echo.lu/legal/en/dataprot /protection.html>). The United States, however, has historically prohibited criminal uses of private information, but attempted to balance individuals' needs with those of industry by permitting some collection and uses of personally identifiable and user behavior information, particularly when the user knowingly consents. Of course, other governmental bodies may have positions similar to one of these approaches, or may go in a completely different direction (for example, denying privacy rights altogether).

At the same time that governments are attempting to safeguard individual privacy online, companies and industries are seeking to gain as much access to user data as they can, given the tremendous value such information provides. Companies in the United States have formed self-regulatory groups that have proposed and promoted guidelines for their members to follow. Although the guidelines have been pro-use, industry is also trying to be sufficiently sensitive to consumer sentiment and government concern to prevent or at least moderate legislation that could create significant reporting and management burdens for the companies.

You might need to know what the guidelines are to use or sell some of the information you collect about users on your site. Even if you're not interested in the information, how do you comply with the ever-shifting legal and regulatory framework? Ultimately, there is no substitute for legal advice and research, but as a first step, it is vital that you create, publicize, and follow a "privacy plan" for your site as well as your business. The Federal Trade Commission's June 1998 "Privacy Online: A Report To Congress" provides the framework for such a plan by setting out its Fair Information Practice Principles:

- notice and awareness
- choice and consent
- access and participation
- integrity and security
- enforcement and redress.

Using these categories as your guide, you can craft a basic plan which fits the needs of your company and its customers, which can then be refined and modified based upon applicable law and the self-regulatory policies of your particular industry. (The current FTC information about privacy, including its reports on online privacy, can be found on the FTC Web site at <http://www.ftc.gov/privacy/index.html>.)

Telling Users How Information Will Be Collected, Used, and Protected

THE MOST IMPORTANT CONCEPT IN RESPONSIBLE USE OF personally identifiable information and user behavior data is notice: tell your customers all the details about how their personal information will be collected, used, and protected. You don't need to give intricate, technical detail. In fact, that may work against you if you are ever accused of misuse of information, because the goal of the disclosure is to make policy clear and understandable to the entire public.

The disclosure statement on a Web site is usually part of the disclaimers, or (increasingly) a separate statement of the site's privacy policy. It is good practice to provide a link to the policy from each of the main pages of the site, which may include the home page, a search page, and any page on which the user is asked to provide personal information (such as a shipping address for goods purchased on the site). A typical privacy statement will have the following elements:

◆ **Identity of the collector.** It may not be entirely clear who will actually be gathering and storing the data, particularly when a site is owned and/or operated by more than one company. Therefore, a clear statement of identity is helpful.

◆ **Disclosure of collection.** Explain what information specific to that user will be stored, and in what form (personally identifiable or anonymous). If providing the information is optional, explain how to opt in or out and the consequences of electing not to disclose the information.

◆ **Purposes of the collection.** What will you do with the information? It may be that you only intend to include it within aggregate statistics in order to benchmark your site. On the other hand, you may expect to use address and name information to create mass and frequent mailings—or to sell the list to another company looking for users similar to yours for marketing another product or service. Some sites state that they will use the information only for the activity then being performed by the user (such as shipping a purchased item, or sending an article from the site to a friend named by the user), and do not intend to retain it. Whatever your intentions, make them clear to your site's visitors.

◆ **Opportunity to obtain and correct information.** This element of a privacy plan is often omitted, but can be the most critical for users. Depending on what data are collected and the type of errors that can occur, an uncorrected mistake can cause the user embarrassment or even credit problems. As a result, it's actually in your company's interest to provide the ability for a user to correct mistaken data, without additional cost to you. To do so, however, the data must be indexed and stored in a way which makes identification, retrieval, and modification of specified people's information possible and convenient.

◆ **Protection.** What steps are you taking to ensure that your privacy plan is being followed and to counter attempted intrusion into your database? While getting too detailed in a privacy disclosure about your protection efforts can put you at risk for both liability suits and hackers, a statement which reflects both the scope and limits of your security coverage will do much to inform and comfort worried users.

Choice and Consent

THE TWO MAJOR APPROACHES TO OBTAINING CONSENT FOR information collection are well described by their names: "opt-in" and "opt-out." Privacy advocates support opt-in, with which a user must affirmatively state willingness to have personally identifiable information and/or user behavior (or any other private information) stored and utilized by the site or third party. Site owners, of course, generally prefer "opt-out," with which the user is included in the data collection unless specifically requesting exclusion.

The mechanisms for both opt-in and opt-out are as varied as Web sites themselves. In some cases, the choice will be presented to the user in the form of a checkbox on a gateway or user registration page, briefly describing the data being obtained and either asking for permission or allowing the user to remove his name from the list by checking the box (this is one place where a link to the site's overall priva-

Crumbling With and Without Cookies

MANY OF THE DISCUSSIONS of Internet privacy center on the use, and alleged abuse, of "cookies." Cookies are nothing more than tiny text files on a user's computer which are written and then read by Web sites (and some banner ads, such as those provided by the DoubleClick network) through a feature of the Web browser software. Cookies allow sites to resolve one of the biggest problems for providing customer service and consistent online experiences—the "stateless" nature of the Web. Because Web communications take the form of back-and-forth messages, rather than ongoing logins, it is almost impossible for a site to identify a user from one request to the next, other than perhaps by an IP address. Unfortunately, since IP addresses are often given out by ISPs at random, the same IP address on two user page requests five minutes apart may come from the same machine, or two entirely different users—generally, a Web server cannot be sure.

With cookies, a site can take the information it does know about a user (everything from the last page the user visited, to a unique identifier, which corresponds to a more detailed profile kept by the site) and store it on the user's machine. The next time that machine makes a request of the site, the site will receive the cookie as well, allowing it to distinguish and remember this user. To prevent abuse, cookies are generally encrypted and browsers prevent anyone other than the originating site from retrieving and/or reading a cookie file. Think of your hard drive as a vault of safe deposit boxes—each site gets its own (very small) box, with a key—you can't necessarily know what the site is putting into the box, but neither can any other box owner. The cookie file represents the contents of the safe deposit box.

Unfortunately for those sites that want to take advantage of the powerful customization and efficiency possible with cookies, consumers have been misinformed about the actual privacy risk posed by allowing cookie files to be written to their hard drives. As a result, many users will either disable cookies entirely or choose to give a cookie-by-cookie acceptance. If your site depends on more cookies than the user is willing to accept, you will lose that user. Therefore, if you wish to use cookies to provide customization, store credit card numbers for easy e-commerce, or just be able to greet your users with the digital equivalent of a wave to a known customer, you need to make sure they understand what cookies are—or, more importantly perhaps, what cookies are not:

◆ They do not search the user's computer for private information stored elsewhere.

◆ They do not contain any personally identifiable information or behavior data which wasn't previously supplied to the site by the user (either explicitly by typing it in, or implicitly through a pattern of activity).

◆ They are not programs, but rather simple text files, and thus cannot execute on a user's machine and potentially cause damage.

◆ They do not generally contain unscrambled credit card or telephone numbers or other such data.

If you are curious about the role and format of cookies, you can read your own machine's cookies file by searching (on a Windows machine) for the cookies.txt file on your hard drive, and reading it using notepad or some other text editor or word processing program. While there are many valid concerns over privacy on the Internet, one of the most-raised, the cookies file, is an example of a minimal invasion of privacy which actually does provide significant convenience and other benefits to users in return.

cy policy may be placed). In others, the choice is implicit—for those sites using "cookies" to track user behavior or identity (see the sidebar on the previous two pages), any user who turns off the cookies feature of a browser (both Navigator and IE support cookie blocking) will essentially be opting-out, and some users may accept or refuse cookies on a case-by-case basis.

Choosing whether to go with an opt-in or opt-out strategy on your site, or some combination of the two, is an exercise in risk assessment. Questions you may ask in making this determination include:

1 How crucial is the collection of this particular information to your site's business model? If it's of particular importance, you may choose opt-out to maximize the number of users whose information will be collected.

2 Who are your users, and how likely are they to object to the collection of information? The greater the chance of objection, the stronger the argument for opt-in.

3 What legal and self-regulatory issues do you need to address in making the opt-in/opt-out choice? For some user populations (most notably children, a subject to be addressed at the end of this chapter) and for some types of information use (such as focused telemarketing or the disclosure of medical data), opt-in is more likely to be mandatory.

Whatever route (or combination) you offer, remember that your ability to rely upon users' consent to collection of information depends on the users being adequately informed before making their choices. In fact, if you fail to describe your plans for the data you collect completely and accurately and problems arise (e.g., you use an e-mail address to send multiple unsolicited advertising messages which crash a server, or provide some names and addresses to a business partner who turns out to be a criminal), your failure might be an additional claim against you in the resulting lawsuit.

Giving Users Access to Collected Information for Review or Correction

THE OVERRIDING PRINCIPLE BEHIND THE REGULATION OF data collection and use is that the information about a person belongs to the person, not to the collector. As a result, most privacy advocates place a great deal of importance on giving users the ability to review the data collected about them, and to make corrections to those data. In the past, consumers have faced this question primarily in the context of credit reports, those collections of purchases, loans, and payments that are used by companies to make credit or even employment decisions. Those companies have been forced by both public outcry and legislation to provide free reports, to make prompt corrections, and to give consumers other remedies in the event of errors.

For a Web site owner the access/participation issues are at the same time easier and more difficult to manage than for credit report companies. On the one hand, most sites are built from scratch, so procedures for tracking and storing personal data can be developed initially. Even if your site has already been launched and includes data collection, the relative youth of the commercial Web means that you may not have a tremendous amount of legacy files to be re-sorted and indexed, and it's likely that most such collection has been done by database software with sorting capability built in.

The downside, though, is that fielding these types of user requests can be time- and labor-intensive, and you need to dedicate personnel (or contract out) to ensure that it happens correctly and efficiently, particularly if the access requirement becomes law rather than policy. Credit tracking companies are typically large and heavily staffed; online businesses tend to be leaner from the outset, and for a company that is simply adding a Web site to its traditional (nontechnological) operations, user access may require actually hiring additional personnel, adding to the cost of operating the site. Another potential negative is that, in the event you have collected more or different information than that stated in your site's privacy policy, fulfilling user requests for access quickly would reveal that inconsistency to the public.

In the end, though, your goal in collecting any kind of user information is to get accurate and usable data. The people whose behavior or statistics you are collecting are much better at tracking down errors than your company would be. Showing an openness to that process and putting a friendly face on it may make your site's visitors more comfortable and more willing to provide detailed information to you in the future. Moreover, if your ultimate goal is either to resell the data to third parties or to increase advertising through better site value, capitalizing on user input to correct mistakes will benefit those efforts tremendously.

Ensuring the Security and Integrity of Collected Private Information

THE SMALLEST STOREFRONT, EVEN A PUSHCART, WILL HAVE a lock to keep unwanted intruders from walking away with the merchandise. It is astonishing, then, that many businesses fail to protect their online assets using even the most basic protection. What kind of "lock" do you need to put on the private information you collect from your users to keep it secure, and to whom do you give a "key"?

Essentially, your obligation is to take reasonable steps such as firewalls and passwords to protect your data files from unwanted intruders or misuse by your own employees, and employ backups and other techniques to reduce the chance of loss. The technical solutions are not the only ones—make sure your internal management structure and procedures support the security effort, from deciding who gets physical access to server spaces (since the easiest way to break into a database is with a floppy disk) to assigning responsibility for periodic audits of security measures. If you are subcontracting out the hosting of your site, these obligations must be passed along in writing to your contractor. Further, if you are sharing information with another company, whether a credit card processor, warehouse, or business partner, include within your contract appropriate obligations on the other party to keep the data secure. A faulty release of data might well be blamed on you as the collector, even if your own security measures were adequate. Keep in mind that, to the extent that your data are particularly sensitive or critical to your business, you may wish to hire "tiger teams" of computer security professionals who will run unannounced sample attacks to detect any holes in your online security measures. If you do bring in a "tiger team," be prepared to be appalled—because so much of Internet technology relies on other elements to work properly, there are many potential inroads into a database collected via a Web site.

Data integrity is a different matter entirely, one that interconnects with the above discussion on access. There are many reasons to verify that your data are complete, unaltered, and uncorrupted, and fit your business needs, and a number of methods for achieving that objective. Beyond getting users involved, or at least offering them that opportunity, it can be helpful to compare your data collection against other publicly available sources. For example, you can run a quick, automated comparison between a name/ address list and a digitized telephone book for pertinent regions. You can also pass credit card numbers through a filter that detects invalid number formats and numbers of known stolen cards. Another good practice, particularly when collecting shipping, financial, or other critical information, is to display all of the user's entries to allow confirmation and/or correction before they are actually submitted to the warehouse or bank.

Neither the security nor integrity efforts discussed here are necessarily easy or inexpensive to implement, but once again, good business practice, industry self-standards, or even law may require them. Too many companies have been the victim of terrible press and loss of good will due to charges of breaches of their data security, particularly involving personally identifiable information (see the sidebar on the following two pages). By the time you correct

LEXIS/NEXIS and the Case of the (Allegedly) Pilfering P-TRAK

EVEN COMPANIES THAT collect and disseminate data online as their main business, such as the online research tool LEXIS/NEXIS, can be the victims of consumer concern about privacy violations. In the summer of 1996, LEXIS/NEXIS introduced its "P-TRAK" database, a directory of individuals' personally identifiable information republished from a large data collection company. The initial version of the database, which was available only to LEXIS/NEXIS's paid subscriber base, included Social Security numbers of the named individuals. However, after a public outcry concerned with the possibility of privacy invasion or fraud arising out of access to the numbers (often used for identification purposes), within a few weeks of the initial launch of P-TRAK, LEXIS/NEXIS removed the Social Security numbers from its available information.

Some months later, a rumor began to circulate around the Internet that the P-TRAK database not only was continuing to publish Social Security numbers but also was including the maiden name of the person's mother (which had

the problem, or learn about the rumors, the damage is already done and irreversible—particularly if the discussion about your company is archived online, and shows up on a Web search some time later.

Enforcement and Redress for Privacy Violations

WHAT HAPPENS IF A USER'S PRIVATE INFORMATION IS collected by you and misused either by you or some other party? Once again, the penalties and liabilities you may face are going to depend on the type of violation, your industry and type of business, the law applicable to the situation, and how much effort you in fact made to manage the data in a never actually been part of P-TRAK). Because the combination of Social Security number and mother's maiden name is frequently used by telephone service representatives to verify credit card or bank customer identity, or to issue new cards or accounts, it is understandable that such a database (if it in fact had existed) could have put a number of people at risk of being victimized by scam artists or other criminals. By the time LEXIS/NEXIS became aware of the disseminated rumors and began publicly disputing them, the scare had already been reported as news by a number of papers and television stations, and had even prompted FTC action to improve online protection of user data. Even today, a Web search for "P-TRAK Mother's Maiden Name" may still turn up tens of sites which either continue warning their users about the alleged privacy violations by P-TRAK, or which have archived their older (and uncorrected) warnings from 1996. (For LEXIS/NEXIS' official statement on P-TRAK and privacy, you may look at <http://www.lexis-nexis.com/lncc/about/p-trak.html>.)

responsible fashion. Still, there are some major categories of potential responses about which you should be aware:

◆ **Self-regulatory actions.** Some industries have established overarching, voluntary bodies which set and enforce policies regulating actions of member companies, whether among themselves or with other companies, or the public. It is quite plausible that, in the event a member company's site is involved in a privacy breach, the aggrieved user may look to the self-regulatory framework to seek damages. Penalties assessed by these bodies may include fines, public admissions of wrongdoing, or commitments to work promptly and diligently to stop the data misuse. While these organizations may not have the authority of law behind them, they can wield significant power among their members, particularly when the group has worked with the government to make self-regulation an acceptable alternative to more stringent legislation. These groups may have one other advantage—their proceedings may not be part of the public record, allowing even a guilty company to minimize publicity about the action.

◆ **Regulatory action.** The FTC and other governmental bodies have a number of different avenues available to them to punish those who violate their rules, including those regarding privacy. From direct sanctions to lawsuits, the liability represented by a government enforcement action can be quite high. Further, while some court proceedings can be private, governmental enforcement actions may be very public, and thus very embarrassing—the FTC, for example, keeps a record of its enforcement activities on its Web site as well as records of past activities and other information at <http:// www.ftc.gov/ftc/formal.htm>.

◆ **Civil litigation.** Depending on the type of misuse, applicable law or court precedent may provide a "private right of action"—in other words, allow the victim to directly sue the violating company for damages in a civil court. Alternatively, if you are involved in a business relationship during which you receive and misuse information gathered by your partner in violation of your written agreement, your partner may sue you for breach of contract and other damage claims. Obviously, an actual lawsuit, with the resultant potential for bad publicity and large-scale damage awards, is significantly more problematic than a self-regulatory hearing, making settlement a better alternative. Remember, too, that one of the elements of a civil litigation is the right to discovery—it's always possible that documents and information produced at discovery may demonstrate a much broader failing by the company, leading to further suits and bad press.

◆ **Criminal conviction.** Some laws may actually provide for criminal liability for the company, or even its executives, for large-scale and serious misuses of sensitive information. Credit card fraud is one obvious example of this, but others may apply to your business as well.

Putting Privacy in Place—a Checklist

THERE IS NO WAY TO ACCURATELY ASSESS YOUR PRESENT
and future risk arising out of collecting and using others'
information via your Web site without competent counsel.
This advice may come from attorneys specializing in privacy
and online business, from trade groups, from government
representatives, or even from your users when they complain about or suggest changes to your then-current data-
gathering procedures. The following checklist should help
you know what questions to ask and where the potential
problems in your company's site strategy might lie.

◆ What are the laws regarding online privacy to which you,
your affiliates, or your business partners may be subject?
What are the potential penalties for disobeying these laws?

◆ Does your industry or that of your affiliates or partners recommend or mandate any particular approach to user data?

◆ What information are you actually collecting on your site?
This may include both obvious places like registration
forms, as well as less-visible collection through e-mail
response forms, online purchases, monitored chats (particularly with logins), addresses collected from comments
sent to the Webmaster, telephone orders from an online
catalog, and the like.

◆ Who within or outside of your organization has any access to
the data you collect? Is this data in aggregate (anonymous) or
specific form? Do you have written agreements with each
party about its use of the data?

◆ What precautions have you taken to keep your data servers
and transfers secure? What written employee and contractor
policies and contracts do you have which supplement these
precautions?

◆ To whom have you assigned responsibility for fielding and,
more importantly, following up on users' complaints about
misuse of their personal information?

◆ Based upon direct communication and other sources (e.g.,
surveys, competitors' reports, news media), what are your
customers' and users' expectations of privacy online? How

sophisticated are they in the use of the Web? Do they understand the facts about cookies?

♦ Do the law, self-regulatory policy, or user expectations require opt-in rather than opt-out selection for information collection? If so, for which kinds of data will you be electing an opt-in approach?

♦ Have you communicated your overall privacy plan to your users? How visible is your privacy policy? Have you made sure not to promise more stringent protection than you can reasonably provide?

MARKETING TO AND HEARING FROM CHILDREN ON THE INTERNET

IF BOTH GOVERNMENT OFFICIALS AND USERS CONSIDER unsolicited commercial messages and privacy "hot" issues, then the topic of Internet users under age 18 is more than hot—it's boiling over.

Children have long been of particular interest to both advertisers and consumer protection advocates, for many of the same (general) reasons:

♦ They are less able to distinguish truth from hype in product and service claims.

♦ They are strong advocates for the products they wish to purchase. ("Can I have it, huh, Mom? Can I, can I, can I, please???")

♦ They themselves are frequent purchasers, especially of smaller items.

♦ They watch/read/listen to a tremendous amount of mass media.

♦ They experience (and give) much peer-to-peer recommendation (and pressure) regarding which products are "cool."

As children's activities have become less supervised, and the amount of commercial media has grown, there have been a number of efforts designed to protect children from inappropriate marketing messages and purchase solicitations. In the United States, this effort has been led through on the self-regulatory side by the Council of Better Business Bureaus, through its Children's Advertising Review Unit (CARU), found online at <http://www.bbb.org/advertising/childrensMonitor.html>. As stated on the site:

"The Children's Advertising Review Unit" (CARU) of the Council of Better Business Bureaus was established in 1974 by the National Advertising Review Council (NARC) to promote responsible children's advertising and to respond to public concerns. The NARC is a strategic alliance of the advertising industry and the Council of Better Business Bureaus (CBBB). It's [sic] Board of Directors comprises key executives from the CBBB, the American Association of Advertising Agencies (AAAA), the American Advertising Federation (AAF), and the Association of National Advertisers (ANA). The NARC Board sets policy for CARU's self-regulatory program, which is administered by the CBBB and is funded directly by members of the children's advertising industry."

The major impact of CARU has come from its Self-Regulatory Guidelines for Children's Advertising (the "Guidelines"), first published by member organization ANA in 1972 and last revised by CARU in 1997. The Guidelines follow a governing set of principles (see the sidebar on the following two pages), which like the FTC's "Fair Information Trade Principles" may provide a useful framework for evaluating the children's issues for your Web site.

The Guidelines, while lacking the direct force of law, are extremely influential. First, the member organizations (made up of the larger advertisers and advertising agencies) have incorporated the Guidelines into their recommended practices as well as their self-regulatory enforcement activities—CARU itself has an enforcement procedure, following that of the National Advertising Division (another BBB organization charged with promoting truth and resolving disputes over advertising claims). Second, because of their

The CARU Principles

FROM THE GUIDELINES <http://www.bbb.org/advertising/caruguid.html#principle >: Six basic Principles underlie CARU's Guidelines for advertising directed to children under 12:

1 Advertisers should always take into account the level of knowledge, sophistication, and maturity of the audience to which their message is primarily directed. Younger children have a limited capacity for evaluating the credibility of information they receive. They also may lack the ability to understand the nature of the information they provide. Advertisers, therefore, have a special responsibility to protect children from their own susceptibilities.

2 Realizing that children are imaginative and that make-believe play constitutes an important part of the growing up process, advertisers should exercise care not to exploit unfairly the imaginative quality of children. Advertising should not stimulate unreasonable expectations of product quality or performance either directly or indirectly.

3 Recognizing that advertising may play an important part in educating the child, advertisers should commu-

prominence, the Guidelines have garnered the attention of official government bodies. The FTC made specific mention of the CARU Guidelines in its June 1998 "Privacy Online: A Report To Congress," stating, ". . . CARU has an enforcement mechanism in place to promote compliance with its online privacy guidelines, and has achieved a remarkably high level of compliance under this mechanism in the offline media over a long period of time. Although CARU has worked to encourage Web sites to adhere to its privacy guidelines with respect to the collection of personal information from children online, to date it has not achieved the same widespread adherence it has achieved in other media."

Why have CARU and the FTC spent so much time and effort on the specific case of online marketing to children, and why would the standards for judging Web site privacy nicate information in a truthful and accurate manner and in language understandable to young children with full recognition that the child may learn practices from advertising that can affect his or her health and well being.

4 Advertisers are urged to capitalize on the potential of advertising to influence behavior by developing advertising that, wherever possible, addresses itself to positive and beneficial social behavior, such as friendship, kindness, honesty, justice, generosity, and respect for others.

5 Care should be taken to incorporate minority and other groups in advertisements in order to present positive and pro-social roles and role models wherever possible. Social stereotyping and appeals to prejudice should be avoided.

6 Although many influences affect a child's personal and social development, it remains the prime responsibility of the parents to provide guidance for children. Advertisers should contribute to this parent-child relationship in a constructive manner.

protection be higher than those of, for example, broadcast television? In large part, this arises out of the uniqueness of the Web and its interactive, anonymous nature. At no time in history has it been easier, and more tempting, for advertisers and marketers not only to talk to but also to listen to minors and to get them involved with ongoing conversations and activities, particularly at such a low cost. Once companies start using the Web, they can reduce their dependence on costly focus groups whose results may be far less authentic than direct feedback and observation of how children actually utilize a Web site in a natural environment rather than in a testing center. Consider, too, that the prevalence of classroom Internet labs opens up not only the home but also the school environment for marketing messages and even online purchases. From the kids' perspective, the online environment is attractive because it allows them not only to be anonymous, but also to be on an equal playing field with adults. It also allows them to impersonate adults, or at least to pursue adult activities and materials that would likely be prevented or monitored under supervision of parents, teachers, or storeowners.

As with general privacy concerns, the protection of children online is likely not to be left solely in the hands of self-regulatory bodies, but will be the subject of governmental action, both in the United States and abroad. For example, the FTC's June 1998 report concluded that whereas self-regulation might work for adults, it would probably be insufficient to protect children absent federal legislation. On July 17, 1998, Senator Richard H. Bryan (D-Nevada) introduced the "Children's Online Privacy Act of 1998" (S.2326), which required online businesses to obtain verifiable parental consent prior to "the collection, use, or disclosure of personal information from children." The bill contains certain limitations and safe harbors, but the general thrust would clearly place a heavy administrative and staffing burden on any site knowingly collecting personal data from those under (in the case of this bill) the age of 16. This bill is neither the first nor is it likely to be the last effort by the U.S. Congress or individual states to legislate the behavior of online businesses marketing to children. Nor is this trend limited to the United States—the European Union has published a number of reports and proposals regarding the protection of minors online, including in the context of marketing. One example is a "COUNCIL RECOMMENDATION of 24 September 1998 on the development of . . . national frameworks aimed at achieving a comparable and effective level of protection of minors and human dignity." (This document may be found online at <http://europa.eu.int/comm/dg10/avpolicy/new_srv/pmhd_en.htm>.)

Once again, it is impossible in a book such as this to give a definitive answer on appropriate and legal methods of marketing to children on the Web—it will depend entirely on the jurisdictions, industry, and marketing plans of your company. To minimize your risks, it is critical to keep the following issues in the forefront of your Web site planning, contracting, and management:

◆ Positively identifying the minors from among the visitors to your site and blocking them when desired
◆ Appropriate methods when you do wish to market to minors
◆ Verifiable parental consent for online retailing to children and granting certain parents' rights.

The Availability and Reliability of Age-Related Blocking

IN A JANUARY 23, 1996, *DILBERT* COMIC STRIP, THE MAIN character proclaims to his canine pal Dogbert that he is developing software to prevent teenagers from accessing pornographic content on the Internet. Dogbert's deadpan reply: "Did you know that if you put a little hat on a snowball it can last a long time in Hell?" Although protective measures for the 'Net may be a bit more effective than that of the snowball's little hat, it is true that the persistence and ingenuity of many teens and even younger children seems indomitable, assuring security meltdown.

Every liquor store and movie theater owner understands that there are many ways for an underage patron to lie or fake proof of age, and many of us know the older-looking kid (or helpful big brother or sister) who used to escort or buy for the little kids. For all the trouble this poses well-meaning businesses in real life, the online equivalent of the "fake i.d." is easier, more serious, and far more prevalent, because on the Internet you can't see or hear the person claiming to be an adult. The only information you are guaranteed to have about the user is that which he or she provides, the truth of which is far from guaranteed. (You'd be amazed how many times Mickey or Michael or M. Mouse from Orlando, Florida, has visited sites that require user registration.)

For some sites, the issue of user age is unimportant—after all, the *New York Times* or CNN.com are not likely to publish any material online which they would not put in their mass-market regular products. Similarly, a site devoted to tourism or technical information is not likely to be deemed harmful to minors. On the other hand, businesses from retail to adult content have a vested interest in determining the actual ages of their site visitors, in the same way that other companies must discover from which country an online customer comes. If you do decide you need to verify age, choosing how much effort to exert and the extent to which you require absolute certainty means balancing the inconvenience to your users against the level of risk you are willing to accept. For example, one highly reliable verification method is a telephone call coupled with enough faxed pieces of identification to form a solid profile of the user. However, few if any Web site users would ever submit to such stringent methods simply to access regular Web site content, except perhaps to sign up for a brokerage account or apply online for a credit card (where regulatory requirements may force such measures).

What other options do you have which, while less intrusive than a document request, may still give you a reasonable amount of comfort about your users' ages? Most sites use a valid credit card number for identification, on the assumption that credit cards will not be issued to anyone under 18, and that the credit card issuers have done enough due diligence to accurately determine age. This is, of course, easier when the site in question offers goods or information for purchase—users will be expecting some sort of credit card check. If your site is otherwise noncommerce related, though, asking for a credit card number will generate suspicion, if not hostility.

Understandably, the sexual content sites have been pioneers in the area of age verification methods. Because providing sexual materials such as photographs to minors can expose these companies to lawsuits or criminal penalties, they have collaborated on a number of age-check "gateways" before allowing users into the body (so to speak) of the site. These verification tools, which may provide single-password access to a variety of sites, all depend on credit card numbers, even if the sites themselves do not charge access fees. These adult-check services, though, are quite closely associated in the public mind with sexual content, and may not be appropriate for other kinds of companies.

The choice for age verification methods is not an all-or-nothing proposition. From credit card to telephone verification to trivia questions about events more than 18 years in the past, your selection will depend upon:

◆ the average (and desired) age of your users
◆ your type of business and the actual risks you would face for dealing with underage users
◆ the value of your content and other online offerings (and therefore the level of inconvenience your users will be willing to accept to prove their ages in order to get at those offerings)
◆ how quickly you need to verify the age and bring your users into the next level of your site.

Responsible and Legal Marketing to Children

MANY COMPANIES PREFER TO BLOCK, OR AT LEAST IDENTIFY, underage visitors to their Web sites. What about those who want to encourage children to come to their sites? In some cases, these may be traditional marketers extending their real-world children's brands to the Internet—breakfast cereal and toy companies are leaders in this area. Others, though, may be online-only companies or traditional businesses taking advantage of the youth-heavy demographics to reach a new audience. Either way, the company must know the "rules of the road" for marketing and advertising to children.

Safe online children-targeted marketing practices grow out of those derived for traditional media, and the CARU Guidelines and similar resources do a good job of stating those. (Keep in mind that CARU defines its protected group as those users under 12; remember that other laws or groups may have a different age floor.) These practices include:

1 Plain-language disclosure of the real odds of prize promotions ("Many will enter; a few will win")

2 Clearly delineating when something is an advertisement (the commercial break on radio and television)

3 Accurate and typical uses of products shown in advertisement, and explanations when something is exaggerated for marketing effect

4 Extra care taken to explain and display safe uses of a product, including showing adult supervision when needed.

Because of the unique qualities of the online marketplace, though, some additional concerns must also be addressed, a fact reflected in the CARU Guidelines, which devote a section specifically to "Interactive Electronic Media." Generally speaking, these include:

◆ **Interactivity.** The two-way nature of the Web can allow you to establish a much closer rapport with children, perhaps using "spokescharacters" (such as Kellogg's Snap, Crackle & Pop or cartoon characters). Your company needs to take extra care that it doesn't provide an advertisement disguised as a club or informational message—"Hey, Suzy, would you like to hear a story about how Sugar Frosted Stars made Fred into an Olympic champion?" This is challenging, particularly when the character is the major focus for your brand identity, and the easiest way to drive traffic to your site. Moreover, even if you don't intend an otherwise entertaining or informative use of your character to be advertising, a regulator or judge, and certainly a parent, could view it as such.

◆ **Collecting and distributing a child's personal information.** As tricky as this topic is when users are adults, the risks increase exponentially when children are involved, and as stated above, the Internet is the easiest medium with which children can hide their age. First, kids cannot legally give consent, however "informed," when you want to collect and/or resell their data, so you must observe additional precautions and may not be able to legally collect or use such information at all. Worse still, even if you do not expressly solicit the information from children, it may still be provided, whether in a public chat ("Hi, I'm Jenny. I'm 13, and I live in La Jolla, California"), in an e-mail message from a young user, or in a personal profile as part of a free e-mail service you offer. In fact, if you don't ask for age information in your site registration or retail process, a large percentage of your data may be collected from underage users. As a result, you may be held liable for unintentional uses of children's personally identifiable information.

♦ **Chat and message boards.** It's very tempting to allow kids to interact with each other on your Web site. Unfortunately, your chat room or message board could easily be co-opted by older kids or adults, possibly even masquerading as children. Imagine the bad press, lawsuits, or other consequences you might face if a predator or other criminal uses information posted by a child on your site to harm the child. Less serious but still damaging to your reputation is the common problem when older children or adults "take over" a message board or chat area meant for children. Time Warner discovered this when the discussion area on its *Batman Forever* movie promotional Web site devolved into postings such as, "Nicole Kidman is Fantastic and Hot!" and other even less child-friendly topics. It's critical that if you decide to offer chats or a public discussion area, you dedicate the personnel and technical resources to watch and (if necessary) intervene in discussions that could expose you to liability.

♦ **Ease of linking.** Unlike the situation with almost any other media, the boundaries on the Internet between different sites can be almost invisible, especially if a site frames other sites within itself. You must decide how to indicate affiliation between your site and those to which yours links, and how those sites' privacy policies (and those of any to which they link, and so on) might negatively impact your juvenile users, and therefore your company. You may choose in fact not to link outward from your site, or only to those other sites whose privacy policies and treatment of younger users echoes your own.

Parental Consent for Sales
and Data Collection

THE ISSUES INVOLVED IN ACTUALLY SELLING GOODS OR
services to children draw from those of advertising, as well
as data collection, and some others concerns unique to the
sales process. First, it is crucial that you let children know
when they are in fact buying something. It's too easy even
for adults to misinterpret an online transaction as something
less permanent. Next, because cash is not practical in the
online world, most purchases will require credit cards or
checks, both of which probably belong to and are funded by
parents rather than children.

The parental notice issue is actually more a parental consent issue, whether you expect to collect information from
children or to go ahead and sell them something. In all
cases, to the extent that the law or applicable policy requires
that consent be granted in advance, it must be the parents or
guardians who provide that consent. As the exposure of children online grows, the number of situations in which you
will have to get parents' consent prior to communicating
with their children is likely to increase.

As you can imagine, the parental consent requirement
has generated a fair amount of controversy among businesses and industry groups seeking to exploit the online
marketplace, because it essentially eliminates most or all of
the benefit of doing business on the Internet in the first
place. What good is a two-way, interactive medium when
the company must wait for some sort of verifiable parental
approval before business? Consider as well the requirement of verifiability. The move toward parental consent is
one of the few broad areas of Internet business in which
someone's actual identity must be verified. It is not likely
that good-faith efforts to obtain parents' approval will suf-
fice. In most cases the laws will require actual approval,
although the mechanism may vary from law to law and
industry to industry.

Unfortunately, just getting consent in advance is not the end of the effort. If you intend to sell to children, you may have to add one more burden to your management and accounting: the ability of a parent to undo a sale after it's complete. This order rejection process, which has little or no precedent outside the Internet, is a direct response to the convenience and speed by which a child can anonymously place an order on a parent's credit card.

This is more than a generous return policy. The way this concept has been described by CARU and legislators, it would permit parents to cancel a sale between order and shipment. If this right is mandated for your company and your industry, you may have to provide for a delay period with your warehouse or fulfillment house, send a copy of the order to the responsible parent, and still comply with FTC and other rules about shipping within a certain time after placement of the order. It won't be easy, and it might even deter you from offering sales to any consumers, since your customers may turn out to be minors. Ultimately, it's critical that you stay current on the requirements and obligations of online businesses that are targeting, or are at least open to, underage users.

Assessing Child-Related Risk for Your Site

HERE ARE SOME OF THE QUESTIONS TO ASK YOURSELF AND your online business partners in order to calculate your site's exposure and plan its response to the risks associated with underage users:

1 Is your site primarily or partially aimed at users under 18? What about those under 12 years of age?
2 Even if you don't intend to get that audience, is your site likely (by its content) to attract such users? Does your site collect any personally identifiable information somewhere within its pages? (Remember that even an e-mail address for questions may constitute collection of information.)

3   Do you ask your users for their ages? If so, is your site pro-
    grammed to track or respond differently to users who claim
    to be under 18?
4   Is your company or your Web site likely to be subject to age-
    related regulation?
5   Does your industry have its own self-regulatory privacy or
    commerce standards for child-focused Web sites?
6   Do you have a reliable means of verifying users' claimed
    ages? Is it convenient for your site's visitors to use?
7   Do you have any public posting or real-time discussions on
    your site? If so, have you designated an employee or contrac-
    tor to act as a moderator to ensure that inappropriate or
    harmful material is removed?
8   If you are required by law or regulation to obtain parental
    consent, have you created the site and business mechanisms
    to do this?
9   Are you prepared, if a parent requests it, to cancel a purchase
    made by a child on the site?

CHAPTER 3

Employee Use of the Internet

A COMPANY POLICY IS THE BEST POLICY

THE FIRST TWO CHAPTERS OF THIS BOOK discuss ways of putting your business on the Internet, and the risks you need to manage when you do. Many companies are likely to be more interested in doing the reverse—that is, bringing the Internet into the office.

Establishing office connectivity to the Internet may take many forms. In the past, a simple option linked employee desktops or an internal messaging service to the Internet via an e-mail gateway. Later, text-based dialup to ISP accounts became generally feasible. More recently, companies have begun connecting either some or their entire workforce to the World Wide Web, either through a dedicated terminal in a central location (such as a law firm's library), from the desktop via a stand-alone modem, or by way of the company's local area network. Depending on the needs of the company and the technical sophistication of its users, other Internet connections (videoconferencing, file transfer, or Usenet news) may be added to the mix as well.

Management must decide who within the organization receives this connectivity, because adding users to an online resource creates significant incremental costs. Typically, the users granted the earliest access include:

◆ Information services personnel, who may need to obtain software updates or support or otherwise remain current on business-critical questions

◆ Managers and client service staff, particularly those with a pressing need to track competitive industry information or to communicate with customers or suppliers

◆ Technically savvy employees, who may even set themselves up with connectivity long before the company officially offers it as an option.

Of these three categories, the third can be the most problematic for your company. Just as these tech-proficient employees are more likely to work around restrictions on loading or saving questionable files, so too might they use company resources in unexpected and unknown ways to obtain connectivity. They are frequently unaware of the cost or inconvenience their methods generate. For example, consider a recent college graduate who is hired as a clerical worker by your company. Comfortable with computers and the Internet, she wants to continue her online friendships and surfing now that she's on the job. If your company does not yet offer connections to its users, she may still be able to connect a modem she's brought from home to an unused telephone or fax line, or discover that your network has unadvertised links out to the Internet for its e-mail gateway and configure her desktop PC to go through those connections to her personal ISP account.

She may not realize that although her home telephone is billed a single small fee for each online call no matter the length, your business phones are charged at a hefty per-minute fee even for local calls, so her eight-hour constant connection can cost quite a bit of money per month. If she instead piggybacks on another connection via your network, the increased data transfer load may be more than you planned for, exceeding your budget and slowing the sending and receiving of business-critical e-mail. Further, she may download software and other materials via her Internet account, bypassing your virus scanning and desktop blocks, which could potentially corrupt her files, do damage to the network application or file server, or even expose your company to copyright infringement liability (or worse). Even if her downloaded software is otherwise harmless, the customization it brings to her system may conflict with the standards you have set for your desktops, making support of her machine (and any others with which she shares her downloaded treasures) significantly more difficult and costly. Also, if this employee decides to damage your company (perhaps because she resents a poor evaluation by her superior who is dismayed by her lack of productivity), the unauthorized link out to the world could allow her to transmit confidential files right off your network to competitors, customers, or the general public.

If the risks associated with a single employee wired to the Internet concern you, consider how much more exposure you face as you fully integrate Internet connectivity into your workforce. Even if you can budget for some of the telecommunications costs, the same issues about downloads, disgruntled workers, and productivity losses remain, magnified a hundredfold. This seeming Pandora's box has deterred many managers and business owners from connecting to the Internet, or has caused them to restrict access to key people. Unfortunately, their legitimate concern may blind them to the very real benefits that properly implemented online access can bring to a business, even down to the lowest level on the corporate organizational chart.

What are these benefits, and how can they be quantified? In almost any company efficiency and savings can be increased by reducing the number of steps a business activity requires and making more information available to decision-makers at all levels. If implemented properly, Internet access can provide these advantages:

- ◆ Secure communications over the Internet using a "virtual private network" can duplicate the functionality of an expensive, leased line-based wide area network, allowing you to link distant or even overseas offices in real-time for the price of the local ISP connection for each office.
- ◆ Targeted research via the Web and Usenet can give you a never-before-available glimpse into the success and failure of your company and its competitors, and an opportunity to hear what your customers (or ex-customers) are saying.
- ◆ Many government and other information sources, ranging from public filings in the SEC EDGAR database (<http://www.sec.gov/edgarhp.htm>) to requests for comment and position papers and court documents, are now available on the Web at no cost, rather than via the expensive retrieval or

online services commonplace just a few years ago. (A useful place to begin U.S. governmental research is the Thomas site maintained by the Library of Congress <http://thomas.loc.gov>.)

◆ By integrating rule-based forms, access privileges, and Internet resources, a host of business processes can now be automated, from requisitioning of office supplies to time cards to maintaining and managing technical support within your company to travel arrangements, all while logging and tracking budget and account information.

◆ Replacing costly overnight couriers and slow and cumbersome fax machines with e-mail for computer-generated documents will lower the cost and improve the speed of moving materials among your offices or between your company and its suppliers or clients. In some cases, even if e-mail isn't feasible, traditional fax machines may be hooked up to an Internet connection to save transmission costs to another Internet-attached fax.

◆ Placing internal documents (such as benefits information and employee rules) online not only guarantees their continued availability to all connected employees, but makes creation and distribution of revised versions a matter of a mouse click rather than a large printing order.

◆ Telecommuting, or just working from home or hotel, becomes much easier when the Internet rather than a long-distance call is your conduit back to the office.

The goal when providing Internet access to your company and its employees, as with any other company resource you may provide, is to ensure that your employees use it economically and only for business purposes. Part of that process involves training, not only in how to use these new programs and features, but also in what misuse can do to the company and to the employee. The most important element of successful Internet integration within your company, though, is the establishment of proper policies covering Internet use.

In this context, the term *policy* covers a lot of ground. Ultimately, it involves writing and distributing "rules of the road" for each type of Internet use, from e-mail to the Web, with some discussion of the penalties for unacceptable online behavior. First, though, you need to decide on proper rules and management for each type of Internet resource available to you. Here's a checklist you can follow:

◆ How does the resource normally operate? Is it one-way or two-way, real-time or delayed, secure or open, identifiable or anonymous? For example, the Web is primarily a one-way broadcast medium, which may be real-time (stock quotes, newswires) or significantly delayed (the many abandoned and outdated Web sites still taking up server space), has both secure (SSL) and open elements, and both site and user can be somewhat identified (if only by IP address for the user). E-mail, on the other hand, is two-way (or really multi-way, given the availability of spam and other mass e-mail techniques), delayed (mail may take some time to make its way to the recipient, and then will sit until the recipient actually checks for messages), usually unsecure (although encryption is available), and the sender can be almost entirely anonymous, while the recipient must be known. Understanding the way a medium operates is critical to deciding which of your employees may use it, and in what fashion.

◆ What are the business purposes served by the resource? Will you be using it for research, communicating with customers, business-to-business communication, or some other reason? Have your vendors or your clients been pushing for you to be accessible to them via the Internet? If so, how? Remember to think not only about the immediate uses to which you will put the particular Internet tool, but possible future uses as well.

◆ Who needs it? Some employees, from analysts to IS to marketing personnel, will be more likely to benefit from Internet access than will general clerical workers (although they, too, might find many helpful ways to use the 'Net).

◆ How much will it cost to open up this resource to your users? You'll need to consider bandwidth (connectivity and telecommunications charges); software licenses; security tools, such as proxy servers and firewalls; user training; and administrative staff. You may choose to standardize on free or low-cost software (such as that bundled with your computers) rather than licensing more expensive but fuller-featured products.

♦ Do you face any risks specific to your company or industry? Law firms, for example, deal with sensitive information for a variety of clients, and carelessness in protecting that information can negate the attorney-client privilege. As a result, many firms have given thought to whether they should connect attorney desktops to the Internet, and whether they want to use e-mail to communicate sensitive information with clients. Similarly, public companies have many more requirements for the disclosure of material information, including that which could come via e-mail or a Web site, than do most privately held firms. Anything put out on the Internet by a public company might even require formal legal review. There are also risks regarding nondisclosure agreements, industry-specific regulations, businesses that (because of their market presence or product line) are of particular interest to hackers and electronic thieves, and others probably unique to your company.

♦ How are your competitors using this resource? The answer to this question includes not only what they are doing that you should emulate, but also the mistakes they are making that you can avoid.

Once you have used these criteria to understand each type of Internet service you can bring into your office, create your policy. Make sure to include both human resources and IS personnel in the process in order to craft a set of rules and procedures that are fair, workable, and consistent with other policies within your company. Remember to include a periodic review of the policy in your plans.

As much as your company might want to absolutely prohibit personal use of Internet resources, this is almost impossible to do. First, it isn't always clear what constitutes "personal use." Casual surfing of the Web may lead some employees to discover new resources that will benefit your business. It could also just provide them with a needed "mental health break" while they remain at their desks, which could improve their productivity the rest of the day. In some cases, skills learned through Internet use themselves will translate into better business results, since self-teaching may be faster and cheaper than hiring a trainer. Additionally, familiarity with how computer networks and search tools operate may make the company's internal network more understandable.

The other major point to consider is how you will detect personal use, even if you can define it. You don't want to read all e-mail received and transmitted by your employees. Beyond logistical problems, such intrusive monitoring (or similar techniques for watching Web browsing and downloads) can generate a "Big Brother" environment antithetical to the one most employers wish to create.

In the end, what most companies do is to create strict formal policies, but reasonable levels of enforcement. This doesn't mean selective enforcement. Targeting only a few abusers of an Internet use policy, particularly those with political or social implications (such as employees using e-mail to unionize), may lead to the company's being sued for discrimination and disparate treatment. What is critical is to have the laws on the books. When an employee does abuse your Internet connection for personal gain or corporate damage, you should be able to bring all of your company's force to bear to stop the behavior and minimize the chances of its recurrence, including the right to terminate the offending worker.

The next sections in this chapter will help you decide whether and how to link your company and its desktops to resources from e-mail to chat to the Web. Whether you decide to connect your entire company at once, do so in stages, or limit access to a few key employees, it's much better to do so in accordance with a policy you research and establish, rather than finding that your employees have already connected themselves in ways that increase your exposure instead of your bottom line.

STEAMING EMPLOYEE
E-MAIL ENVELOPES

ANALOGIZED UNSOLICITED COMMERCIAL E-MAIL TO
an unlikely delivery discount at the post office and an incredibly burdensome recycling law. In a similar vein, consider the features of this imaginary business courier service:

◆ Its delivery people pick up and drop off at the desktop twenty-four hours a day, but will not carry anything that won't fit in an envelope.

◆ Delivery time ranges unpredictably from two minutes across an ocean to four days to the neighboring building, and paying extra doesn't help.

◆ Depending on how much you are willing to pay the service, its personnel will come to your offices with a knapsack, hand cart, minivan, or tractor-trailer to pick up and deliver your packages. The smaller the container, the longer it takes to deliver all your mail.

◆ The service's envelopes look exactly like inter-office mailers, so documents intended for colleagues occasionally get taken by a courier and delivered to people outside your company who have similar names.

◆ The courier occasionally covers your company's desks, chairs, and filing cabinets with chain letters, penny stock solicitations, and pornographic images and ads.

◆ Some of your employees feel free to use this courier service to send out their Christmas cards, photos of their kids, joke books, screenplays, church newsletters, and résumés, all of which the service accepts without comment (and at your company's expense).

No reasonable businessperson would hire a courier service that fit this description and would terminate a vendor who began exhibiting any of these tendencies, except, of course, for the one "courier" with which almost every company works or is considering: Internet electronic mail for employees.

E-mail, more than any other technology, contributes to the unrealized hope for the "paperless office," with the claim that with the right e-mail tools and accessories, printers and envelopes can become almost unnecessary. In practice, though, the utility of e-mail must be balanced against significant technical and behavioral hurdles.

Identifying and Establishing the Best E-mail Network Architecture

FROM A TECHNICAL SIDE, YOU NEED TO ASSEMBLE BOTH proper software and reliable service providers and integrate them into your existing business systems in order to make effective use of business e-mail:

1 How much e-mail traffic can you expect? The answer to this query will direct how much bandwidth you arrange for your company. Underestimating can result in delays, and overestimating may mean overpaying. Remember to include not only outbound but inbound messages. Also, the type of files being sent will have a great impact on the speed and reliability of your e-mail connection: mostly-text is a much lighter load than are sounds, pictures, or especially video attachments. If e-mail traffic will share a "pipe" with other Internet use, that other use must be factored in.

2 What e-mail features do you need and want? Choosing e-mail software that can send and receive a variety of formats is important. If your business demands accurate tracking and forwarding of messages to the right people, detailed and flexible filtering is a must, and form-generation can help you automate your intra-office procedures. Security needs may require easy-to-use encryption tools, and if you have a mobile workforce, you'll want mail servers accessible via the Web or software allowing easy exchange of mail between PCs and devices such as 3Com's Palm organizer. If you are standardizing across international offices, you may choose a software package that has multiple language versions (although you should make sure that all can be centrally managed).

3 What e-mail sending and client software are others in your industry using? Beyond helping you match any competitive advantage they might have found, their choice may reflect a

Legal Use of Encryption Across Your Enterprise

NO MATTER YOUR BUSINESS, your employees will share information and documents that could damage you if they reached competitors or the general public. While e-mail, like almost all Internet communication, is generally secure owing to the way it is broken down into packets, there is always the chance that, through accident or malice, a message might end up in the wrong e-mail box. One way to ensure that incorrect recipients will not be able to read it is to use encryption tools on both ends of the transmission.

As discussed in Chapter 1, the security level of encryption software depends on the number of possible keys, generally described by "bit" amount. Commonly used levels include 40-bit (2^{40}, or 1,099,511,627,776 keys), 56-bit (2^{56}, or 72,057,594,037,927,900) and 128-bit (2^{128}, or an incredible 340,282,366,920,938, 000,000,000,000,000,000,000,000). The higher the number, the more difficult it is for an intruder with access to part or all of a message to randomly guess the unlocking code. In addition to protecting Web transactions between browser and server, encryption technology may be used to scramble sensitive or private e-mail messages. In some cases, this functionality is built directly into the e-mail program; there are also add-on encryption tools that integrate directly with popular e-mail software.

needs analysis applicable to your company, too. You may even want to collaborate with your competitors, if feasible, to pressure the software vendor to add or improve features particularly beneficial to your field.

4 Does your internal IS staff have sufficient knowledge to implement, integrate, and train your users on the new e-mail system? If not, will you need the software vendor to

Whether and how to use e-mail encryption is not a simple decision. The U.S. government has long considered encryption technology to be of potential use not only to legitimate businesspeople but for terrorists and other criminals, and has classified encryption as "munitions." As a result, it has been difficult, if not impossible, for a company to export heavy (greater than 40- or 56-bit, in many cases) encryption software, either to customers as part of a product or even to international offices in conjunction with standardizing software. It is critical that you check the current status of the law before sending any encryption software beyond U.S. borders. Some firms have worked around U.S. laws by obtaining foreign encryption software and importing it into U.S. offices, but even then, a close check of relevant law and regulations is essential.

Unfortunately, encryption can be co-opted by employees to hide personal communications from corporate monitoring, or even to scramble critical data files to damage or blackmail your company. It is difficult, if not impossible, to introduce encryption without enabling negative use. If your company decides to make encryption available to its staff, it should add language to its e-mail policy (see "The Elements of an E-Mail Policy" on page 202) dealing with the permitted and prohibited uses of encryption software.

supply required services, or are consultants available who would be able to support your company?

Once your company has completed its investigations, the answers can help you shape an RFP (request for proposals) which you can send out to vendors. Even if you are doing all acquisition and implementation in-house, filling out the above checklist would be a useful reference for you and your colleagues both before implementation, and afterward as a benchmark of how the system you've selected fulfills your goals.

Exposure from Employees' Use of E-mail

E-MAIL IS QUALITATIVELY DIFFERENT FROM THE "SNAIL MAIL" and fax machines that preceded it in the workplace. First, e-mail is usually connected to the same computer networks that house much of a company's sensitive information. As a result, an employee can attach anything—from the corporate payroll (as depicted in a 1998 IBM commercial) to a confidential deal memorandum to your wholesale price list—onto a message and send it out to a friend, a colleague, or a reporter in a matter of seconds, without ever having to risk being seen at the printer or the fax machine. Similarly, incoming mail may also have access to the network, potentially exposing your company to virus programs and to having information on your network that is illegal for you to possess—from child pornography to business data from a competitor—without your knowledge or consent (see the sidebar at right). There are also employee e-mail uses that, while short of breaching confidentiality obligations or violating criminal law, can harm and embarrass your company.

One major culprit is misdirected e-mail. It is frighteningly easy to send a message to the wrong recipient. Even if the sender realizes the mistake two seconds after clicking "send," few if any e-mail systems allow message cancellation once it is transmitted. Imagine that the message is one sharply critical of your company's biggest customer, but instead of forwarding the customer's latest unreasonable request to a colleague, your employee instead sends both the request and his lambasting response right back to the customer's CEO. You will be dealing with an unhappy account, if not an ex-account, within a matter of minutes.

Similarly (and perhaps more common), in the case of a multiperson online discussion, a private reply to one participant may instead be sent to the entire list. Depending on the

Siblings' Employers' Rivalry

IT IS NOT SURPRISING that your company might be put at risk by a disgruntled current or former employee using the Internet or plain old-fashioned sabotage. What's amazing about e-mail, though, is how easily a disgruntled employee of another company can accidentally draw your business into the conflict.

Imagine that your company had an employee whose brother happened to work at a competing firm. When the brother becomes unhappy at his job, he takes his revenge by e-mailing to his sibling some confidential information belonging to his employer, the other company. The mere receipt of the information by your company (by virtue of its being stored on your e-mail server) could be considered a criminal violation of the Economic Espionage Act of 1996, 18 U.S.C. § 1831 et seq. (1996), whether or not your company intended to obtain the information, if certain other conditions of the law were met.

contents of that reply, any number of consequences may descend on the sender, intended recipient, and even their employers. The misdirection problem is made worse by a feature of many popular e-mail programs that automatically matches a typed name with an e-mail address from the composer's address book. There may be people with similar names within the address book, and a note meant for John Jones may instead go to James Jones (whose name comes earlier in the alphabetical list). When a single program and address book services the internal and Internet e-mail systems, this can cause company messages to go out to the world and vice versa.

In most cases, an e-mail message is considered "in writing," and e-mail is often stored long after it has been read and may exist on backup tapes months or years after both sender and recipient delete the note (as Oliver North found to his dismay). To the extent that an e-mail message sent from or within your company contains a serious allegation or slanderous accusations, or otherwise violates applicable law, the offended party and law enforcement officials may be able to use it against you much more easily than had the same offensive message been said in a telephone call. It's also much easier to distribute a rumor or outright lie to hundreds or thousands of recipients using e-mail rather than telephone, ground mail, or fax machine, greatly increasing the damages awarded to an injured party. [The Federal Trade Commission devotes a fair amount of space on its Web site to discussions of e-mail fraud and abuses (see <http://www.ftc.gov/bcp/conline/pubs/alerts/doznalrt.htm>).] Even an otherwise personal message sent by an employee (such as a variation on the "Make Money Fast" chain letter that pervades the Internet, or an advertisement for a home-based business that makes fraudulent claims about a product or service) using your company's system might bring you into a private or governmental enforcement action, perhaps long after the employee has left the company.

To maximize the chances that your e-mail connection will benefit rather than devastate your business, it's crucial that your company both make and enforce a proper e-mail usage policy for your employees.

The Elements of an E-mail Policy

SOME FIRMS HAVE WORDY EMPLOYEE MANUALS COVERING every aspect of worker life, and an e-mail policy will likely become another tab in the binder. In other places, a more informal code of conduct is described, perhaps during a new-hire orientation, and may be reinforced with a written handbook or intranet page describing proper use of resources including e-mail. Small businesses may not have a written policy at all. Whatever your corporate culture and practice, though, your company should explain and publicize the following points to all e-mail users:

◆ **Company e-mail is only for business purposes.** It's useful to give positive and negative examples as a nonexclusive illustration of the policy: "Please do not give your work e-mail address to friends or family to contact you other than for work-related matters. Also, you should not put your work e-mail address as a contact point for any online shopping or similar services, nor should you subscribe to e-mail discussion lists for hobbies or private interests with this address. If people do start sending you personal notes to this account, please let them know that they should use another address or, if you don't have a personal e-mail address, contact you in a different way outside the office."

◆ **All company e-mail is the property of the company, and may be monitored to ensure the system is used for business purposes.** This is a crucial point to make, and one that is frequently ignored or resented by employees. It means that anything created on the company system or using its connection (if an employee is out of the office) is the property of the company not only for copyright purposes, but for review as well. In most cases this is both a matter of law and policy, but stating it to employees prior to their use of the service makes it more likely that the company will be able to enforce this doctrine if necessary. (See page 205 for a discussion of monitoring pros and cons.) It can be helpful to remind any unhappy employees that the company pays for the software, hardware, connection, and support that makes the e-mail service possible. Many employees would be surprised to hear what their "free" e-mail is costing their employer.

◆ **Any e-mail message from the company's domain may be assumed (or legally held) to be the official position of the company, with all the liability that may entail.** Even mandatory disclaimers on messages such as, "The preceding message may not reflect the opinion of my employer," may not be sufficient to prevent bad will or legal action against the company for a statement made by an employee in a mail note.

◆ **Double-check every address before sending a message. . . then check again.** Even with this warning, mistakes will happen, but the more the policy can emphasize this risk (together with some horror stories, real or hypothetical), the less likely employees will be to send messages incorrectly.

◆ **Do not use e-mail for sensitive or legal materials without checking with a company manager and/or counsel.** There are a number of reasons for this, ranging from the increased exposure in the event of misdirection to a later discovery request that could pull copies of any messages from the sender, the recipient, or either's backup tapes. Unfortunately, for all its seriousness, this is often the most difficult policy item to implement, particularly in time-critical situations like acquisitions when materials are being sent and received by a number of parties both inside and outside of the company. Still, it is imperative that you educate those employees handling sensitive materials and create a chain of authority for quick decisions about whether to use e-mail or not.

♦ **Do not infringe copyrights or other proprietary rights by e-mailing materials without getting the permission of the author.** If you can't find the author, don't send it. It is a little-known but nonetheless important point that almost all e-mail is protected by copyright from the moment it's created—any author can in theory prohibit another user from forwarding the message. In reality, most authors will never assert their copyrights in e-mail, in part because most e-mail does not have the same commercial value that, for example, this book does. On the other hand, there is a tremendous amount of e-mail forwarding of articles, jokes, images, and videos—almost anything that can be digitized. This is not only a copyright infringement, but (depending on how large the forwarding list and the commercial value of the material being passed along) may even represent a criminal copyright violation, one just as likely to be imputed to the company (with its deeper pockets) as to the individual, even if such individual can be found.

♦ **Under no circumstances should any of the following, if received via e-mail, be forwarded, particularly by non-technical personnel, without careful verification:** warnings of new viruses such as those that can propagate through e-mail; chain letters; appeals for donations of any kind; or stories that a friend's friend swears are true. E-mail users, particularly ones with online friends, will receive dire warnings about the Good Times virus or pleas to send cards to Craig Shergold, probably multiple times. (By the way, a British boy named Craig Shergold did in fact have a brain tumor and did request and receive enough greeting cards for a world's record back in 1990, but the publicity led to an American millionaire paying for the successful removal of the tumor soon afterwards. Unfortunately, the request has continued and mutated over the years, and the Make-A-Wish Foundation and similar groups continue to be inundated with literally hundreds of thousands of greeting cards, business cards, and other materials sent by innocent well-wishers.) The Internet and especially e-mail have allowed many rumors, misunderstandings, and out-and-out hoaxes to perpetuate themselves long after the original creators have gone on to other, perhaps more productive, pursuits. People often forward these warnings or solicitations with the best motives, feeling they are protecting their acquaintances or doing a good deed, but the result is a large volume of useless and even costly e-mail. For anyone who wishes to verify the accuracy of a virus warning received via e-mail, a good place to start is the Computer Incident Advisory Capability site of the U.S. Department of Energy, found at <http://ciac.llnl. gov/ciac/CIACHoaxes.html>. Urban legends from poor Craig Shergold to a $250 chocolate chip cookie recipe can be researched, and debunked, at the Urban Legends Reference Pages at <http://www.snopes.com> or the Alt.Folklore.Urban newsgroup's home site at <http://www.urbanlegends.com>.

The Rights and Risks
of E-mail Monitoring

ANYONE WITH PROPER ACCESS TO THE COMPANY'S COMPUTER network can read any e-mail message coming in or going out to the Internet. As a result, determining whether Steve Smith is sending a price quote to a customer or a résumé to a competitor is as easy as scanning his e-mails.

Just because this is technically simple, however, does not make it an optimal approach. A large corporation can have literally thousands of messages flowing through its system every day, making manual review impossible. Small and large companies alike may wonder whether reading employees' e-mail is even legal. One can easily imagine privacy arguments comparable to those made by people whose phones were tapped or letters opened.

The good news for U.S. business owners and managers is that, by and large, it is legal to monitor employees' communications in the workplace. In a number of cases throughout the United States, employees who protested when their bosses read allegedly private e-mail were rebuffed by the courts on the grounds that the e-mail system is the property of the company and meant for company business only, and that the company (as owner) was permitted to ensure that its resource was being used properly.

For the most part, employees are understood not to have a right of privacy in the workplace, particularly in regard to a company-wide e-mail system. It is noteworthy, though, that in most of the cases and commentaries that come down on the side of the employer, the employer has published an e-mail policy stating that employee e-mail may be monitored. It is also important that, before you implement any sort of e-mail monitoring, you check with the current laws in the state or states in which you operate. Connecticut, for one, passed a law in 1998 (known as Public Act 98-142, "An Act Requiring Notice to Employees of Electronic Monitoring by Employers") that mandates written notice to all employees prior to an employer engaging "in any type of electronic monitoring," subject to certain limited exceptions (see <http://www.cga.state.ct.us/ps98/act/pa/pa percent2D0142 .htm>).

The legality of monitoring is not your company's only concern. E-mail is often felt to be a particularly private activity, even when employees know (or should know) that the system is meant for business. Employees who would never discuss customers or coworkers on the telephone or around a water cooler will do so in an e-mail message to a colleague. A lovestruck staffer will send steamy electronic notes to a spouse or significant other. Both types of messages can be devastating to the sender and recipient if publicized or read by management. There are few things other than layoffs that are worse for morale than a feeling that management treats employees without respect. Monitoring e-mail can quickly become a rallying point for dissatisfied workers.

Should your company monitor e-mail? Most employers will not as a rule read every message sent or received by their staff. However, it is crucial that in your e-mail policy you reserve the right to do so, since there may be cases in which your business depends on learning the contents of an e-mail sent over your system. You may also wish to put filtering software on your server to automatically watch for risky communications (for example, your chief competitor's domain name, or unusually large file attachments).

Once a potentially suspicious message has been flagged, a manager aware of both the stated policy and the risk issues may wish to review it and, if it turns out to be damaging to the company and in violation of the policy, to take appropriate action.

By the same token, any employee who is illicitly monitoring others' e-mail without authorization (whether an IS technician or a curious manager) should be admonished and, if necessary, denied access to the e-mail files. It's important to prevent abuses that could incite employees and interfere with the necessary monitoring the company wishes to do.

THE DOWNSIDE OF DOWNLOADS

LIKE E-MAIL, WEB ACCESS HAS MANY LEGITIMATE BUSINESS uses. But staff access to the Web or other downloads, such as file transfer protocol (FTP), opens up the door to data, software, and documents that can harm the company.

The business risks associated with improper Web use and downloads include serious human resources issues as well. Web browsing and surfing by employees, and the distribution and display of files retrieved from the Internet, can lead to claims of discrimination or sexual harassment, criminal investigations, and multimillion-dollar infringement actions. The types of online use that are most likely to generate liability:

- ◆ Downloading copyrighted material
- ◆ Online gambling and other crimes
- ◆ Obtaining illegal material
- ◆ Displaying or distributing harassing materials.

INFRINGEMENT

AS NOTED ELSEWHERE IN THIS BOOK, THE WEB SENDS COPIES of every file on a Web page to each machine as the page is requested. Most legal scholars understand this to mean that under U.S. copyright law Web users have been granted an "implied license" from the site owners to make that copy, at least for the purposes of viewing the page on a computer screen.

This notion of an implied license assumes, however, that the designer of the Web page has the legal right to grant licenses to the page's content, and that the only use will be for a one-time viewing by a single individual. What happens, though, when materials are included within a Web page to which the page's owner does not have licensing rights, and when users save Web-based files onto a hard drive and reuse or redistribute them? Some copyright holders send cease-and-desist letters to each infringing site that they find. Those holders will tell you, though, that their letters are often ignored; new sites are established faster than they can send more letters out. Most owners of pirate sites are young, often students with few assets against which a large record or television production company or software publisher can seek damages.

What many aggrieved copyright owners do instead is to work with others in their industry to enforce their rights against larger offenders, preferably those with deep pockets—in other words, the corporate world. The software industry has been aggressive in its tactics, especially following the formation of the Software Publishers Association (now the Software & Information Industry Association, or SIIA). The SIIA's Web site at <http://www.spa.org/piracy/pirnews.htm> is filled with press releases about litigation against small and large businesses that have illegally copied software. Many times investigations are instigated by reports from disgruntled ex-employees. Often, the executives at the target company were not aware of the illegal software use until the subpoena or search warrant arrived at their desks.

Today, in addition to copying software illegally, employees are using their multimedia networked PCs to play the latest albums or watch digitized versions of last week's *South Park* episode, and even to post their favorite files on the network server for everyone to view. It's a frightening scenario. Large companies have difficulty auditing every file on every computer. Small firms can be seriously damaged or even bankrupted by the award in an infringement action.

THE DANGEROUS MIXING OF CASINOS AND CUBICLES

HISTORICALLY, IT WOULD HAVE BEEN DIFFICULT FOR EMPLOYEES to conduct high-stakes betting from their desks on a regular basis. But now we have the Web.

Online casinos are proliferating as entrepreneurs exploit the ease of credit card use online and the ability to reach potential players during their workday. Some countries and regions, including New South Wales, Australia, and the islands of St. Martin and Antigua, have been courting online casinos, promising freedom from regulation in exchange for a portion of the profits. A search of Yahoo! will locate Web sites promising video poker, slot machines, real-money sports books, with others offering games of chance and random number lotteries (Interlotto, based in Liechtenstein, is a long-standing example of this: <http://www.interlotto.li>).

Regulators such as the U.S. Congress and state attorneys general have not ignored the growth of online gambling, which threatens not only the economic health of citizens but tax revenues derived from lotteries and casinos in states that permit them. Many legislatures have passed laws banning or restricting online gambling, and attorneys general from Minnesota to New York have brought successful lawsuits against casino operators who permit local citizens to participate in Internet gambling against state law.

Companies may find themselves in the middle of these battles because (as with infringement) the company providing the Internet connection for the gambler may be the biggest target within reach. Further, you can imagine an impoverished spouse going after a gambler's employer because it failed to prevent the gambler from losing his life's savings at the office. Another danger lies in many online casinos requiring players to download proprietary software— a virus or other harmful application could unwittingly be installed onto your company's network.

Illegal Activities on the Web

BESIDES GAMBLING, THERE ARE CRIMINAL ACTS IN WHICH your company's employees can participate while logging on to the Web. The SEC has been cracking down on stock fraud perpetrated by misleading other online investors about a stock in a chat area, an activity that may affect even your own company's share price. Employees with options may try to boost the stock price with insider information or outright lies posted to investment sites (see the sidebar at right).

The FTC takes a dim view of misleading or fraudulent claims about products being sold through Web sites, and your colleague may be managing such a virtual store over a lunch break. Another area of abuse involves pedophiles who have learned to practice their "craft" by assuming false identities online and luring their underage victims via chats to meetings after hours.

Illegal activity is one thing—what about illegal materials? Certain types of documents, images, and other information are not only unlawful to produce, but illegal to have at all. Child pornography is a prime example. Because today many people have their primary and fastest Internet access at work, and because so much material, including illegal material, is available anonymously and conveniently online, employees are using company systems in record numbers to download questionable items.

Child pornography is not the only type of material which is illegal to download, and whose mere presence can cause a company embarrassment or prosecution. In some cases, specific types of information have been interdicted for public

PairGain—Hot Tip or Hoax?

ONE SUCH FRAUD in early April 1999 related to a publicly traded telecommunications company called PairGain. According to news reports, a false press release on a Yahoo! chat room stated that PairGain would be acquired by another company, ECI Telecom. The false release contained a link to a Web site that appeared to be a financial news service operated by Bloomberg L.P. (the parent company of this book's publisher), but that, in fact, was an unauthorized fake of the real Bloomberg site. The stock jumped more than 30 percent before news of the fraud could circulate. A week later, a PairGain employee was arrested and charged with securities fraud. PairGain management was not implicated in the allegations.

policy reasons, such as 128-bit encryption algorithms. The export controls for encryption have been described as prohibiting any kind of export, from shipment of disks containing encryption software to a T-shirt on which an encryption algorithm is reprinted. If your employees access your computer network outside of U.S. borders (either in a foreign office, or via a dial-up from a hotel room or conference center overseas) and download a high-level encryption program or any software containing such programs, they may be breaking the law, and the computer that they are utilizing could theoretically be seized for evidence. Obtaining some types of military-related information (nuclear weapon technology, designs for super-computers, and even instructions for making explosives) can be illegal without proper authorization. In the aftermath of the 1995 Federal Building bombing in Oklahoma City and the Columbine High School massacre in 1999, the U.S. Congress made it illegal to transfer or receive bombmaking information via the Internet, even though the same information may be freely and legally gotten from almost any public library.

Addressing such risks can be tricky. Many downloaders will not know that the file they've requested, or the Web page they're reading, puts them at risk of arrest or even imprisonment. Others will know, or perhaps should know, but differentiating them from innocent downloaders can be a matter for a jury rather than a staff manager. Further, a company that discovers illegal materials on its servers or users' PCs may be under a legal obligation to report the illegality and to bring authorities into the picture, whatever the potential impact on the company's reputation or the possibility of criminal prosecution of the company may be. In the event something like this occurs at your company, it is a very good idea to get advice of counsel knowledgeable both in employment and criminal legal issues.

HARASSMENT CLAIMS ARISING OUT OF WEB USAGE

SO FAR, THE CONFLICTS AND THE RISKS DISCUSSED IN THIS section have been between the employee and the company, or the employee, company, and law enforcement officials. There is one more major area of exposure about which every executive must be concerned: disputes and claims among employees, most notably those of sexual harassment. The types of activities and statements considered harassment are becoming more diverse and more numerous—from the White House and Congress to the local factory or firm.

One trend relevant to anyone connecting employees to the Web is the claim that material downloaded and distributed or displayed by others is harassing and demeaning. The most familiar context for this is pornography. The stereotypical pin-up calendar in the mechanic's office has evolved into the photograph or video file stored on an analyst's hard drive and shown to a colleague who may not appreciate it. Racial jokes, cartoons, and even political messages may be considered harassment as well.

Some very large companies and institutions, including Morgan Stanley, CompuServe, and even Harvard Divinity School have been publicly embarrassed by reports of employees accessing sex sites. Still others have disciplined or fired employees found to be downloading sexually explicit files (see the sidebar at right).

WWW or XXX?

IN 1996, in a very well-publicized report, Nielsen Media Research reviewed the site logs of *Penthouse Magazine*'s Web site to see from which domain names the majority of their users were coming. The results were quite embarrassing for companies like IBM, Apple Computer, and AT&T and for agencies like NASA, all of which found their domain names on Nielsen's published list of the top Penthouse.com visitors.

Nielsen's disclosure was a wake-up call for many executives who suddenly understood that sites could distinguish their users from others, and that their employees were viewing smut on company time and at company cost. A number of authors linked the Nielsen report with the contemporaneous story of how Compaq fired twenty staffers for accessing sexual imagery at work (see Cheryl Currid's September 1996 *Windows Magazine* article at <http://www.winmag.com/library/1996/-0996/09a03002.htm>). It's also not surprising that Pearl Software, in the course of marketing its Cyber Snoop corporate Web monitoring product, referenced the Nielsen report in a white paper available, ironically enough, on its Web site <http://www.pearlsw.com/csnoop3/corpwp.htm>.

Harassment is in the eye of the beholder, the complaining employee. It may be difficult for a business to determine which types of downloads might be harassing. What happens, for example, when you are informed by a systems administrator of some potentially harassing material found on a hard drive during routine maintenance? Do you delete the material? Preserve it for potential litigation? Reprimand or fire the offending employee? Taking overly aggressive action may be unnecessary, and could even expose your company to claims by the downloader for infringement of privacy or (if fired) wrongful termination. Failing to take action upon notice, though, could worsen your company's position if a harassment suit is in fact brought against you. Like many other human resources questions, a Web use policy in place ahead of time will provide valuable guidance.

Filtering Risk from Your Company's Browsers

THE GOOD NEWS ABOUT WEB AND DOWNLOAD RISKS, AS COMpared to e-mail, is that a much greater level of control is possible for your company without imposing unduly on perceived privacy rights of employees. With downloads, third party materials are being limited, filtered, and even monitored—the employees are just recipients. Technological tools for watching or blocking Web sites and downloads are available and easy to use, albeit with some caveats.

Whatever approach your company takes, from open browsing to a carefully configured proxy server (hardware and software that can keep all but specific Web sites from loading at the desktop), a policy should be a major part of your tool set. Here are elements to keep in the forefront of your company's plans:

1 What business purposes do you wish to achieve by giving employees Web and/or FTP access? This may differ among groups of workers: internal analysts may need broader access to news and information Web sites, IT staff will need easy download ability for updates and technical support, and inventory managers may have to do business-to-business transactions online. You may also be combining outside Internet access with documents or programs available on your company's corporate intranet, including human resources documents that must be available to every employee.

2 How much bandwidth can you afford? The smaller the total Internet "pipeline" being shared by your staff, the more limited are the downloads and graphic-intensive or video-filled Web sites. You may wish to restrict large downloads to after hours, or arrange all file transfers above a certain size through the IT staff, who can balance bandwidth needs. Remember to calculate not only the outside bandwidth load, but how employee Internet use may slow down your internal

network—too much browsing could interfere with printing or application servers sharing the same Ethernet wiring.

3 Do you want to monitor employee Web use, and if so, do you have the human and technological resources? While the software for capturing site requests is fairly easy to operate, the log files generated can be huge. Finding the right tools to parse and digest the files for easy sorting can be a drain on an already overworked IT or HR department.

4 What software will you provide to your users? From a risk management perspective, your choice of browser or file transfer software will be driven by the level of controls each product gives you. If you want to block certain sites or customize the interface, find the browser that meets your needs best. You may be able to acquire or create custom versions of browsers through value-added resellers or consultants.

5 What software and controls are others in your industry using, and what have been their experiences? As with e-mail software, shared knowledge can lead to combined negotiation power with vendors.

6 What will your company do when its policies are disobeyed? If the company may be liable for a copyright infringement or harassment suit, or even costly bad publicity, a harsh response may be merited. Merely wasting time by following a personal stock portfolio, though, could simply warrant a spoken warning or an internal note in an HR folder.

If a staffer objects to company monitoring or restrictions, remind the employee that the company would not be expected to allow everyone free use of a television, video game console, and library of magazines along with an ever-present group of friends. The company provides the privilege of Internet access; it can also exercise the right to remove it.

CHAPTER 4

Protecting Your Company

INSURING AGAINST ONLINE RISKS

OR MOST COMPANIES, "RISK MANAGEMENT" means liability insurance. Business people know that not every risk is avoidable, nor is it always the best idea to completely eliminate risk even if you can. When economics or practicality require risks, or if a single occurrence could bankrupt you no matter the prevention efforts, liability insurance companies can cover many of your financial obligations.

If your company is like most, it has some sort of insurance covering general malpractice (if yours is a service firm), injury or death to employees and customers, and fire and theft damage and loss. Beyond that, there will be coverage specific to your industry: advertising and creative agencies carry errors and omissions policies against intellectual property or privacy infringement and failure to pay guild or talent fees; pharmaceutical firms have broad-based coverage for unforeseen side effects from medication; airlines must insure against cargo damage and passenger deaths or injuries from mechanical failure and even terrorism; electronics retailers buy insurance to back up extended warranties. It's often said, and largely true, that any risk is insurable—for the right fee.

When it comes to putting your business online, though, your insurance is probably not sufficient to cover the type and scope of new risks to which the company may be subject. Insurance brokers who are not well educated in the business aspects of the Internet may not be able to guide you through the process or know of carriers who offer appropriate policies. Instead, you will often find yourself leading your broker through an evaluation of what your company is doing, what it means, how much exposure you are likely to face, and (most importantly) how to reduce that exposure through proper insurance policies or riders.

Searching for Appropriate and Affordable Coverage

YOU AND YOUR BROKER SHOULD LOOK FIRST AT THE NEW policies insurance companies are creating for and marketing to Internet development and services companies. Insurers targeting this market segment include AIG, USF&G, and Chubb. Within each of these policies (which may be called computer, technology, or cybertech liability insurance) are a number of different types of coverage and/or endorsements, only some of which your company may have:

◆ Copyright and trademark infringement in Web site content
◆ Breach of privacy
◆ Advertising errors and omissions
◆ Copyright infringement in underlying computer programming, be it object code or source code
◆ Errors and omissions covering technical problems that result in business losses for the covered company or its customers
◆ Fraud protection
◆ Patent infringement and/or enforcement (in some policies; others specifically exclude these types of damages)

Unfortunately, these policies may not be sold generally to businesses within your industry, and therefore the carriers may not have pricing for the type and size of your company. In other words, if you want to buy the coverage, the carrier or agent may not know how much to charge you, and therefore may not sell it to you. Even if the carrier is willing to provide you with a cybertech policy, it may charge you a price higher than that for all of your other insurance, even if it represents only a small part of your company's total business, because the risks are so difficult to quantify.

If your current carrier doesn't have any sort of cybertech policy in its product line, it may be difficult to obtain add-on Internet business coverage. You could find yourself having to purchase two full liability policies, the traditional one and a new-media-focused one, in order to get appropriate coverage, leading to much higher fees and administrative costs, and disputes between the carriers in the event a claim is made.

If you're lucky enough to have an insurer with a new-media policy, your risk manager may not have the knowledge to accurately answer the risk assessment audit questions posed by the carrier. If an incident occurs that was not clearly described in the questionnaire or other information gathering, the carrier may deny coverage. As in the situation described earlier with your insurance broker, you may not be able to depend upon your standard internal risk management channels to provide you with appropriate guidance.

Identifying Sources of Risk from Online Activities

WHAT RISKS ARE YOU LIKELY TO FACE? THIS INQUIRY MAY BE viewed as a set of building blocks, from the simplest online presence to the most complicated and risky:

BANNERS AND OTHER ADS

ONLINE ADVERTISING IN ALL ITS VARIED FORMS (SEE CHAPter 2 for more details) is the simplest way to put your business online. Whether your ad stands alone or is connected to your company's own Web site by means of a clickable banner, or whether you're advertising on some other Internet resource (such as a newsletter or mailing list), the type of insurable risks you face with Internet advertising are close to those confronting advertisers in traditional media. They include:

1 Making false or misleading advertising claims, whether about products or prices
2 Misuse of copyrighted material or trademarks in the body of the ad (or, in the case of a banner ad, within any software programming included to make the advertising more interactive or to add animation or sound)
3 Exploitation of talent without appropriate compensation (such as within a stock photo used as the background of a banner)

4 Modifications to your advertising made by the site owner or list owner on which the ad is placed.

Of course, since the advertising is on the Internet, any insurance you obtain must cover not only domestic but also international risks, such as violations of advertising laws in other countries. If a policy doesn't cover cross-border liability, whether for advertising or any of the other types of exposure discussed below, find out ahead of time, so you can make contingency arrangements.

WEB SITE LIABILITY CONCERNS

WHEN YOUR COMPANY ADDS A WEB SITE, THE EXPOSURE picture becomes murkier, because the number and types of activities that can take place on a Web site far exceed those for a simple online advertisement. The situation is similar to renting a storefront compared to buying space on a billboard or in a newspaper. Whereas a banner ad might contain one photo, a Web site might have a copy of your company's latest television commercial, complete with famous actors, well-known background music, and effusive statements about your product which are only partly backed up by research. Although the commercial may enjoy only a limited run on television, it can remain available on the Web as long as the file stays on your server, adding to the likelihood that one of the depicted actors or other involved parties will discover that the international digital rebroadcast and synchronization rights (required by most guilds for Internet usage) were not part of the original commercial production agreement.

Here are few other risk categories which you cannot afford to overlook:

1 Online retailing. If you are selling anything online, particularly if you accept orders from outside the United States, you must concern yourself with supplier delays, misshipments, damage in transit, and credit card and other payment fraud. Although because of encryption Web-based transactions are quite safe from casual interception, the distance and anonymity of Web users make it difficult to detect and combat stolen credit card usage or other consumer fraud.

2 **Online communities.** Chat and public discussion forums can expose your business to claims of personal and trade libel, securities fraud, or even contributory liability for physical injury (if two participants meet after an online chat and one harms the other)—situations not covered under traditional liability policies .

3 **Specialized information services.** If your company is one that faces potential lawsuits based upon its expertise (the case for attorneys, doctors, financial services businesses, or consultants), you must take care not to provide any information that could be regarded as "advice." Even with taking such precautions, though, a court could find that a particularly detailed answer to an e-mail question, if incorrect or misleading, could be considered malpractice. Enhanced coverage may be necessary for such possibilities outside the realm of traditional malpractice insurance.

Geographic issues play a large part in Web site insurance questions. Many business insurance policies will cover only the United States, or just your business's physical offices. With the Web, not only are you communicating all over the world, but many companies contract with hosting firms to establish their Web presences, and may locate their sites on multiple, mirrored sites for speed and backup. If the "server farms" are not in the geographic coverage of an insurance policy, claims that arise out of Web-based business activity may not be covered.

INTERNET USE BY EMPLOYEES

SINCE CONNECTING YOUR COMPANY'S STAFF TO THE INTERnet can be as much of a change in how you do business as establishing a Web site, it's little wonder that the question of adequate coverage comes up in this context as well. The good news is that your firm's existing liability policies are more likely to cover employee Internet use, since it occurs within your office with your company's equipment, than they would be for Web site problems. It is possible, though, that some online exposure may remain outside your existing covered risk categories:

1 Criminal liability for online gambling, transmission or receipt of child pornography, or industrial espionage (whether or not authorized) using the Internet

2 Trade libel or securities fraud arising out of statements made by staffers in online discussions

3 Intellectual property infringement via online copying and distribution of protected materials

4 Business interruption and lost sales when a relied-upon Internet connection to suppliers or sales channels fails, or when a competitor, disgruntled ex-employee, or malicious user exploits a security gap in your company's Internet link to do damage.

In order to determine whether or not your company's existing policies fall short, it's not enough to read the categories of coverage. Have someone familiar with policy language examine the definitions of terms such as *damage* and *equipment* very carefully, including how each term is used throughout the policy. If this review highlights any ambiguities, make sure to get clarification from your carrier *in writing,* so you will know what additional coverage your company may require.

Sharing the Risk Management Burden

GIVEN THE INTERDEPENDENCE AND INTERCONNECTIVITY required to successfully do business on the Internet, it is crucial to verify that your online business partners (Web developer, hosting company, software vendor, warehouse, shipping firm, bandwidth provider) all have sufficient insurance to cover themselves and you in the event that their failure generates damages. Having a standard "minimum insurance coverage" provision in your form agreements, which includes being given a copy of the contractor's insurance certificate and having your firm listed as a "named insured" on any relevant policies, is a good first step. Nothing can replace, however, serious due diligence of and inquiry into the risk tolerance and management of the other companies.

Unfortunately, you may find that one or more of these other companies is underinsured for these types of risks or, worse still, has no relevant insurance in place. This is a particularly common problem with some start-up Web technology companies, many run by young entrepreneurial Web specialists who may not have the business experience to understand the need for insurance. Ironically, these same firms raise the strongest concerns about reliability and long-term financial strength, risks for which insurance is most appropriate.

If you find that a vendor is under- or uninsured, or if you are not comfortable with relying on the other company's insurance, there are a few additional steps to take. First, examine whether the firm's activities on your company's behalf are already covered by your policies. If not, you may be able to buy a rider or endorsement that includes the Internet project and/or the contractor. Be sure to include the cost of such coverage as a credit against any fees you must pay the contractor. If you cannot add the other company to your policies, your inquiry and the questions it raises may well give the other party a head start on discussing and obtaining coverage with its own carrier.

FINDING APPROPRIATE PROFESSIONALS

MOST BUSINESSES WILL NOT HAVE ALL OF THE IN-HOUSE technological and global talent necessary for a successful Internet implementation. You will most likely outsource some or all of your Internet development and maintenance to technology shops, advertising agencies, consultants, or traditional IT outsourcing firms.

The first section of this book described the dealings you are likely to have with such firms and the contractual and other issues you and they will have to work out together. There are resources on which you can draw to narrow the field for potential alliances:

1 Check with your company's existing vendors (advertising agencies, computer consultants) to determine whether they offer Internet services, or whether they will act as your contractor with other companies and under what terms.

2 Speak with your clients and suppliers who may be ahead of your own company on Internet issues. With whom have they worked, and how would they rank their satisfaction?

3 If you are seeking a Web designer, spend some time browsing sites in your industry and related fields, assuming the role of your company's customer. Which sites work best? Which features impede rather than improve Web site usage of the type your site will likely offer? If you cannot identify the designer of a particularly attractive site, ask the site owner. (Remember, the site designer may or may not be responsible for ongoing maintenance and revisions—make sure the party whose name you get actually produced the site whose features you admire.)

4 If you are not part of your company's IT staff, employees within that group may already be speaking with colleagues at other firms about these questions. Check to see what they have learned.

5 Consider whether your company is better off using one of the larger, national or even international Web design firms for your site and hosting needs, or whether a smaller shop will give you better attention and service. The bigger shops may have access to higher technology and, if your business is multinational, may be able to provide or contract for localization services as well as initial development.

6 Try to obtain RFPs (request for proposals) used by other companies for Web development, ideally including the names and responses of the firms that answered the request. Even if you can't get the results, the questions themselves will give you guidance for your own search.

This process of locating and hiring technology service providers is fairly straightforward. The more difficult question, though, is how to find nontechnology professionals to help you specify, assess, and manage these efforts once you have chosen a firm to implement them. These professionals include attorneys, accountants, customer service personnel, insurance agents, and sales managers. The last thing you want is to sit down with your lawyers before drafting the Web development contract to explain what Web chat is, or to have your accountant tell you that he does not understand why international concerns are raised by an online mall.

The first question you should ask any proposed adviser is, "Do you use the Internet in your own business?" If the other company does work on the Internet, it may have faced some of the same issues your company will, perhaps gaining some wisdom it can pass along to you.

Here are some additional questions you might ask professionals:

ATTORNEYS

1 In what Internet-related transactions and/or disputes has the attorney been involved? Did the firm represent the customer or service provider, or has it had both types of businesses as clients?

2 What relevant specialization does the attorney offer? An effective Internet or new-media lawyer will have a strong grounding in contracts, as well as familiarity with copyright, trademark, and licensing, since everything contained within a Web site is by definition intellectual property. Depending on the particular type of Internet use, knowledge of retailing, real estate, advertising, or securities law can also be helpful.

3 Has the attorney developed relevant form agreements that you can modify for your needs? Beyond the cost savings involved in using pre-written model agreements, you can also gain some comfort that an often-used contract has been vetted and tested for reasonability and coverage of likely problems.

4 Is the attorney familiar with technical jargon? Contracts should include programming language and technical features for accurate descriptions, so that you can show exactly what service is expected. Overly vague language makes charges of noncompliance of contractual obligations difficult to prove.

ACCOUNTANTS

1 Has the accountant advised clients on issues such as sales tax for online sales, international retailing, and amortization of hardware and software? How familiar is the accountant with the relevant state and federal (and perhaps even international) regulations concerning Internet accounting principles?

2 If yours is a public company, are your auditors allocating an appropriate amount of risk to your online operations? Firms inexperienced with the realities of the Internet may assume too much exposure is present, or fail to properly reflect contingent liabilities that do exist. Valuation of an online business unit is also tricky, particularly given the inflated market price for many Internet businesses. Has the accountant done valuations for the sale of such businesses?

BUSINESS CONSULTANTS (E.G., SALES ANALYSTS, MARKET RESEARCHERS, PRODUCT DESIGNERS)

1 Do they understand the current demographics of the Internet? What about the likely changes to those demographics?

2 What techniques do they have to deal with the heightened expectations of Internet-based consumers (speed of response, availability of information)? How have they addressed situations of bare-margin online competition? How have they addressed situations of bad will spread via message boards or e-mail by disgruntled customers or competitors?

3 Are they sensitive to international issues, from language to culturally acceptable advertising?

4 If your company hopes to save significant money and/or generate higher profits by moving its operations online, what can the consultant do to bring your customers onto the Internet and into your Web site?

ARCHITECTS/OFFICE MANAGERS

1 How can you design office space to enhance Internet connectivity, telecommuting, and network security without compromising aesthetics or the potential for staff growth?

2 What kind of furniture and equipment can most affordably ensure productive computing while minimizing the likelihood of carpal tunnel syndrome and other repetitive stress injuries?

Epilogue

CLICK HERE TO FINISH

THE OFT-REPEATED MESSAGE OF THIS BOOK IS A
simple one: putting your company on the Internet
and bringing the Internet into your offices require a
great deal of thought and management. Hasty action,
failure to realistically assess risks, or not taking the
Internet as seriously as you do the rest of your
business can have unforeseen and often serious
consequences. This note of caution, however, must
not overshadow the other message of *Clicking
Through*—the incredible power of Internet technology
to make your company more competitive, broader-
based, and smarter. Using the checklists, analyses,
and approaches contained in the preceding chapters
will go a long way toward helping you reap substantial
savings and earnings from your online investment.

The Internet is exciting precisely because its
constantly developing capabilities create opportun-

ities daily, not only with high-powered stocks, but also by improving everyday business operations and finding new sources of revenues. How can you spot situations in which Internet and/or intranet applications can give you a business advantage? Look for opportunities wherever:

◆ Information stored on your business's computer systems is frequently edited, printed, duplicated, and sent out. This would include annual reports, bills, forms, and brochures.

◆ Information or documents stored on your company's computer must be provided to a business or customer who will ultimately retain it on another computer. Invoices, inventory figures, receipts, contracts, content sharing, and customer data often fall within this category.

◆ Certain informational queries are asked often and answered in the same or similar way each time. Examples of this include customer service questions; requests for product specifications, documentation, or forms; and news bulletins or press releases.

◆ Your company needs to integrate subsidiaries, offices, or employees who are widely geographically spaced, including business travelers and telecommuters.

◆ You want to explore or commit to a new type of business, or create a temporary alliance with another company, without incurring the costs of acquiring additional real estate or creating new print advertising and collateral material.

◆ Customers need access to a great deal of widely dispersed information (e.g., federal, state, and local taxation decisions, opportunities for new business), which is difficult and time-consuming for an individual to collect.

What if you are only beginning the process of identifying and pursuing these types of opportunities? Given the amazing amount of business already happening on the Internet, including perhaps by your competitors, you may feel that if your company hasn't yet "jumped into" online business, or hasn't gone beyond a simple "brochureware" Web site, it's too late. Never fear: instead of being intimidated, look at the delay as an advantage. Not only does a later entrant into cyberspace get to study the successes and failures of those businesses that have preceded it online, but also it can create an online presence or build online access services that serve the Internet user of tomorrow. Of course, you can't afford to build and forget; unless you constantly reevaluate your own strategy and implementation, you're likely to be overtaken by a company that waited longer than you did!

A further point is worth noting: beyond all the potential problems outlined in this book, your biggest hurdle to successfully and profitably bringing your business online may not be legal or even technological, but cultural. Many businesses look upon the Internet as the "Wild West," an unknown frontier not "ready for prime time," where rules don't apply and laws cannot protect. Hyperbolic news stories about Internet predators, fears about credit card and other types of fraud, as well as inexperience using the Internet help to fuel this fire. A powerful way to combat these fears and to convince your worried colleagues that the cost/benefit analysis falls firmly on the side of adding the Internet to your company's business strategy is to sit them down in front of a high-speed Internet connection, with a few carefully chosen bookmarks/favorite places to explore, and close the door. The epiphany that often occurs once someone actually tries to use the Internet for business, coupled with the demonstrated effectiveness of the risk-management strategies contained within this book, may well turn your opponent into your staunchest ally.

Above all, don't get caught in the trap of thinking that the Internet is just the World Wide Web, or that there's only one way to use the Internet for business. The Internet is not a technique or device but a communications medium, one with astonishing flexibility and opportunities for business that have barely begun to be tapped. Just as the standards and connections of online technology have conquered geographic boundaries, so too will imaginative and well-planned uses of the Internet by companies such as yours break down economic barriers, industry hierarchies, and the rules of business, which are seemingly impossible to challenge in the traditional world. As a result, instead of the assumptions about costs and risks which arise out of the brick-and-mortar business environment, the commercial Internet generates one overarching assumption: anything and everything is now possible.

Webliography

NOTE: Web sites mentioned in *Clicking Through* are referenced in the index by an underlined page number following the company name.

This "Webliography" lists sites that are the first places to look for new rules, resources, tips, and techniques. Most of these should be part of your Bookmarks or Favorite Places files on your Internet browser:

Government Sites

GOVERNMENTAL AGENCIES AND OFFICES, FROM LOCAL TO national and even around the world, have leapt on the Internet as a way to disseminate information, documents, forms, and new regulations. Each locality and agency may have its own page, but here are a few major places to begin searches:

◆ **THOMAS** <http://thomas.loc.gov>. Run by the Library of Congress, the premiere site for finding U.S. federal and state governmental resources. Search by governmental branch, law name and/or numbers, and state names.

◆ **Information Society Project Office** <http://www.ispo. cec.be/>. An initiative of the European Commission responsible for various electronic commerce and other matters; the **Legal Advisory Board of the Information Market** site <http://www.echo.lu/legal/en/labhome.html> is another good resource for EC technology information.

◆ **Federal Trade Commission** <http://www.ftc.gov>. The U.S. agency responsible for advertising and marketing regulation; site contains many useful bulletins, links to relevant law, announcements, and forms.

◆ **National Telecommunications and Information Administration** <http://www.ntia.doc.gov/>. This agency of the **U.S. Department of Commerce** <http://www.doc.gov> publishes domestic and international telecommunications and information technology information.

◆ **Congressional Internet Caucus** <http://www.netcaucus. org/>. Described as "a bi-partisan group of over 100 members of the House and Senate working to educate their colleagues about the promise and potential of the Internet"; a good starting point for learning about Internet-related legislation.

Internet Basics

◆ **Whatis** <http://whatis.com>. Among the best sources for definitions of online/technology terms, from abacus to Zmodem, including links to relevant Web sites.

◆ **Yahoo!** <http://www.yahoo.com>. A fast, extremely well-organized index site, Yahoo! groups Web sites into categories and allows both hierarchical (category) and name searches, as well as offering shopping, chat, games, and free e-mail; **Excite** <http://www.excite.com>, **Lycos** <http://www.lycos. com> and **Infoseek** <http://www.infoseek.com> are similar. **CEO Express** <http://www.ceoexpress.com> is a well-regarded portal to all kinds of information useful for businesspeople.

◆ **Google** <http://www.google.com>. Although less well known than its older rivals **Hotbot** <http://www.hotbot. com> and **Altavista** <http://www.altavista.com>, Google is among the fastest and most relevant of the true search engines, allowing text and other types of searches within the contents of a Web page.

◆ **Netscape** <http://home.netscape.com> and **Microsoft** <http://www.microsoft.com/windows/ie/default.htm> are the beginning places for users of each of the two popular browser programs; other browsers include the small and fast **Opera** <http://traviata.nta.no/opera.htm> and the superfast text-only **Lynx** <http://lynx.browser.org>, and information about all popular browsers can be found at **BrowserWatch** <http://browserwatch.internet.com>.

♦ **CNet** <http://www.news.com>, **ZDNet** <http://www.zdnet.com> and **Internet.com** <http://www.internet.com>, along with **Hotwired** <http://www.hotwired.com>, are useful top-level sources for Internet-related news stories, as well as links to other Web sites' articles; Internet-related software can be researched and downloaded at **Stroud's Consummate Winsock App List** <http://cws.internet.com> (for Windows), and **Tucows** <http://www.tucows.com> and **Download.com** <http://www.download.com> for multiple platforms.

If you're looking for an Internet service provider, **The List** <thelist.internet.com> and **Boardwatch** <http://boardwatch.internet.com>, two sister sites, are good starting points. Finding a good Web or software developer is a bit harder, given the sheer number and different qualifications you'll need; sites such as Earthweb's **Developer.com** <http://www.developer.com>, trade associations including the **World Wide Web Artists' Consortium** <http://wwwac.org> and **New York Media Association** <http://www.nynma.org> (both based in New York), and directories such as those maintained by **SoCalTech.com** <http://www.socaltech.com>, the **Association of Internet Professionals** <http://www.association.org>, **SiliconAlley.com** <http://www.siliconalley.com>, **The New Media Guide** <http://www.newmediaguide.com>, and **Constructors** <http://www.constructors.com> may help your efforts.

General Business Information

Hoovers <http://www.hoovers.com> is a useful source of basic information about companies and industries—advanced data is available to paid subscribers. Others such as **EDGAR Online** <http://www.edgar-online.com> and the **Dow Jones Business Directory** <http://businessdirectory.dowjones.com/> may provide further helpful direction.

To find more detailed sources for your industry, start with Yahoo! or one of the other indices discussed above. Type in your industry and start clicking through the many links that will appear. If you are looking for a particular company's site, and can't find it via Yahoo!, try the **Real Names** <http://www.realnames.com> directory, which you can search by company name and slogans. **PR Newswire** <http://www.prnewswire.com> can help you track news and developments for your customers and competitors alike, as can business news providers such as **Bloomberg** <http://www.bloomberg.com> (the parent company of this book's publisher) and the **Wall Street Journal** <http://www.wsj.com> (subscription required). As for other ways to contact companies or individuals, telephone and reverse directories such as **Anywho.com** <http://www.anywho.com>, **BigBook** <http://www.bigbook.com> and **BigYellow** <http://www.bigyellow.com> can be invaluable aids.

For business travel, check to see if your company's travel agent has its own site. If not, or if you need more powerful searching and/or booking capability, you may choose from a myriad of Web sites such as **BizTravel.com** <http://www.biztravel.com>, a business-focused company that tracks frequent flier mileage and offers other helpful services; **TheTrip.com** <http://www.thetrip.com>; **Travelocity** <http://www.travelocity.com>; or the many airline sites. Land-based travelers can use **Mapquest** <http://www.mapquest.com> to get door-to-door driving directions. (You can even get archived satellite images of anywhere on earth, courtesy of Microsoft's **Terraserver** <http://www.terraserver.microsoft.com>!) To check out a city or even make reservations for dinner before you arrive, look at local guides such as Microsoft's **Sidewalk** <http://www.sidewalk.com> or those found on **Yahoo! Travel** <http://travel.yahoo.com>.

This list is by no means complete, nor could it be. Further, the links may change due to technical issues, business combinations, or reorganizations, or even sites dropping off the 'Net. Therefore, check this book's own site <http://www.clickingthrough.com> for an updated version of this guide. And keep clicking through.

Index

NOTE: Underlined page numbers indicate Web site addresses.

243

Government sites, 235–236

R

251

About Bloomberg

FOR MORE SMALL BUSINESS INFORMATION AND RESOURCES, visit the Entrepreneur Network at Bloomberg.com—featuring business tips, feature stories, audio and video commentary, and more—at **www.bloomberg.com/business**.

Also watch *The Bloomberg Small Business*™ television show every Saturday at 6 A.M. on the USA Network and DirectTV.

Bloomberg L.P., founded in 1981, is a global information services, news, and media company. Headquartered in New York, the company has nine sales offices, two data centers, and eighty news bureaus worldwide.

Bloomberg Financial Markets, serving customers in 100 countries around the world, holds a unique position within the financial services industry by providing an unparalleled combination of news, information, and analytic tools in a single package known as the BLOOMBERG PROFESSIONAL™ service. Corporations, banks, money management firms, financial exchanges, insurance companies, and many other entities and organizations rely on Bloomberg as their primary source of information.

BLOOMBERG NEWS℠, founded in 1990, offers worldwide coverage of economies, companies, industries, governments, financial markets, politics, and sports. The news service is the main content provider for Bloomberg's broadcast media, which include BLOOMBERG TELEVISION®—the 24-hour cable and satellite television network available in ten languages worldwide—and BLOOMBERG® RADIO™—an international radio network anchored by flagship station BLOOMBERG® RADIO AM 1130 in New York.

In addition to the BLOOMBERG PRESS® line of books, Bloomberg publishes *BLOOMBERG®* Magazine, *BLOOMBERG PERSONAL FINANCE*™, and *BLOOMBERG® WEALTH MANAGER*.

About the Author

ROBERT RODE

Jonathan Ezor is a noted expert on computer and Internet business and has been involved in the area since the beginning of the commercial Internet. For the last several years he has given presentations on Internet risks and opportunities all over the United States, including Internet World shows in Chicago, Los Angeles, and New York, PLI and other legal seminars, and Sun's JavaOne Expo in San Francisco. Co-author of *Producing Web Hits* (IDG Books, 1997), Mr. Ezor has been a regular columnist on legal issues for *Business-Week* Online and the *@NY* electronic weekly and has written on Internet and computer legal topics for *Advertising Age* (which named him a "Web Warrior" in 1995), the New York New Media Association, and *Infoworld*. He has practiced new-media business and corporate law and is currently director of legal affairs for Mimeo.com. Mr. Ezor has been interviewed on Internet and business by the *Wall Street Journal*, the *New York Times, FOX Business News,* and many trade publications.